fish behavior:
why fishes do what they do

by dr. helmut e. adler

Front cover:
>   (top) Siamese fighting fish (*Betta*) x paradise fish (*Macropodus*).
>   Photo by H.J. Richter.
>   (bottom) Kissing gouramis (*Helostoma temmincki*).
>   Photo by H. Hansen.
>   (right) Sabre-toothed blenny (*Plagiotremus tapeinosoma*).
>   Photo by Dr. G.R. Allen.

Back cover:
>   Lizardfish (*Synodus variegatus*). Photo by A. Power.

ISBN 0-87666-162-2

Distributed in the U.S.A. by T.F.H. Publications, Inc., 211 West Sylvania Avenue, P.O. Box 27, Neptune City, N.J. 07753; in England by T.F.H. (Gt. Britain) Ltd., 13 Nutley Lane, Reigate, Surrey; in Canada to the book store and library trade by Clarke, Irwin & Company, Clarwin House, 791 St. Clair Avenue West, Toronto 10, Ontario; in Canada to the pet trade by Rolf C. Hagen Ltd., 3225 Sartelon Street, Montreal 382, Quebec; in Southeast Asia by Y.W. Ong, 9 Lorong 36 Geylang, Singapore 14; in Australia and the south Pacific by Pet Imports Pty. Ltd., P.O. Box 149, Brookvale 2100, N.S.W., Australia. Published by T.F.H. Publications Inc. Ltd., The British Crown Colony of Hong Kong.

CONTENTS

A bottom-dwelling triglid, a sparid and a common European eel in a grouping that might be found in cool Atlantic waters. Note the partially hidden fish in the picture. Photo by Dr. D. Terver, Nancy Aquarium.

A community tank of blue gouramis, *Trichogaster trichopterus*; kissing gouramis, *Helostoma temmincki*; tiger barbs, *Capoeta tetrazona*; and bala sharks, *Balantocheilos melanopterus*. Photo by Dr. D. Terver, Nancy Aquarium.

Chapter I

HOW TO STUDY BEHAVIOR

What is behavior?

Take a quick glance at a well-established aquarium! It will repay you with the pleasing sight of flashing fins and a colorful, but at first confusing, picture of fishes moving back and forth or up and down or resting at the surface, in the middle regions or on the bottom of the tank. A longer look will reveal individual patterns of swimming, preferred rest positions and interaction of one fish with another. *You are now observing behavior* and you are doing so under almost ideal conditions, because the healthy aquarium is least affected by all the disturbing influences that interfere with observing captive animals. Its closed little world is often not much smaller than the natural habitat where tiny or highly sedentary fishes live and, in any case, the larger and more active fish species are unsuitable for aquarium

Saltwater aquarium displaying colorful reef fishes set up by Warren Tom of Honolulu, Hawaii, shown here with his family. Photo by Dr. Herbert R. Axelrod.

Angelfish (*Pterophyllum scalare*) interacting. What are they saying to each other? Photo by Klaus Paysan.

culture. For information on the behavior of these kinds of fishes we must rely on the reports of ichthyologists, fish collectors, commercial and sports fishermen, skin divers and aquanauts, who seek out their subjects in their natural habitat.

We observe behavior because it is fascinating and entertaining. Aquarists are often found staring at their fish tanks, as if hypnotized, and people are happy to pay entrance fees to observe fishes in public aquariums. We can also study behavior with a more serious purpose, by selecting various bits of behavior and recording them under specified conditions. By changing conditions and noting the changes in behavior that follow, we can ultimately manipulate the behavior of our subjects in accordance with principles that have emerged from previous observations. Finally, by contrasting different conditions, we can often find some rule that governs the particular behavior we are studying.

After much checking of our facts and long hours of observation, we are at last convinced that we know why a fish is doing what it does. What we mean is that when we watch our angelfish grabbing each other by the jaw and testing each other's strength, this behavior will end with the selection of a mate and spawning on a leaf or other suitable spot. We decide this activity is part of the mating pattern. So when we claim we know why a fish is doing what it does, we really mean that we have had the opportunity to watch one particular kind of behavior that is regularly associated with some other type of activity. The why of behavior refers to a relationship then, not to some experience or feeling that we assume the fish to have and that causes it to behave in a certain way.

This restriction in meaning helps us to avoid the trap of explaining behavior by essentially human characteristics. Fish are fish. It also helps us to keep in mind that an explanation that merely consists of naming a certain kind of behavior does not advance our understanding of it.

We must learn not to ask why, but to ask how!

Good observation will show us that each pattern of behavior is the result of some previous history. Part of it is due to the environment. There is the physical environment, including such factors as the temperature, oxygen, pH, and the size and arrangement of the tank, as well as the social environment of other fishes of the same and differing species. There is also the organic development of the fish, its maturation due to physical growth and the functioning of its organs, such as the fins and gills, the nervous system and the brain. Finally there is the personal history of each individual, made up of the specific influences of environment and organic development in their natural interaction on this one individual. It is the key to understanding its behavior.

Ultimately, the goal of observation is the complete description and classification of fish behavior. This knowledge may lead to prediction and control of certain kinds of behavior and may serve useful purposes for the aquarist, the fish culturist and the fisherman. It may, in the end, help the cause of conservation and an understanding of the ecology of the aquatic environment. On another level, behavior may be related to its underlying biological and physiological functions. This approach serves to deepen the understanding of the biological basis of behavior, as well as contributing to the study of evolution and the theoretical analysis of behavior. The analysis of behavior is a task for the professional scientist, but it also is an area in which the serious aquarist amateur may make a significant contribution.

What is a fish?

It may appear a little far-fetched to try to explain what a fish is, but it might repay us later to take a brief look at how scientists classify fishes.

Of all animals with backbones, fishes are the most numerous. There are at present

Some fishes have skeletons made of cartilage: (Left) A huge manta ray, *Manta birostris,* looming over a school of goatfish, some gaterins and damselfish, photo by Pierre Laboute; (top right) a blue spotted reef ray, *Taeniura lymma,* photo by Dr. Herbert R. Axelrod; and (bottom) an adult zebra shark, *Stegostoma tigrinus* (grows to 11 feet in total length), photo by Pierre Laboute.

Beluga or white whales (*Delphinaptera leucas*) being fed by hand at the New York Aquarium. Belugas are the most vocal among whales and the species most often heard by man. Photo courtesy of the New York Zoological Society.

some 20,000 known species, although guesses range as high as an eventual total of 40,000. For comparison, there are at present a total of some 8,600 known bird species and 4,500 species of mammals.

Whales and porpoises live in the water and have fins, but they are warmblooded creatures and suckle their young; thus, they are mammals. Fish, on the other hand, are coldblooded, their temperature is essentially that of their environment, their body is usually covered by scales instead of hair, and, with a few exceptions, they breathe by means of gills. Then there are shellfish, such as oysters and clams, as well as lobsters and crabs. They have no backbones and thus are not fish at all.

Three major classes of fishes may be distinguished. The jawless fish (Class: Agnatha), comprising the present-day lampreys and hagfishes, are related to many ancient and now extinct species. The modern sharks and rays (Class: Chond-richthyes), with their skeleton made of cartilage, make up another group that was once represented by a much larger number of species than it is now. By far the largest modern class is made up of the bony fishes (Class: Osteichthyes), which includes all the well-known aquarium fishes. The more advanced bony fishes are often referred to as teleosts, a grouping that excludes such specialized forms as lungfishes, coelacanths, sturgeons, gars and bowfins.*

* A note on scientific nomenclature: CLASSES are subdivided into ORDERS with scientific names ending in '-iformes' and sometimes further divided into SUBORDERS with the suffix '-oidei.' ORDERS are made up of FAMILIES with names ending in '-idae' (subfamilies terminate in '-inae'). Each species has a binomial designation, the first term is capitalized and denotes the GENUS (plural: GENERA), the second the SPECIES (plural: SPECIES). Both names are *italicized*. Single italicised terms therefore denote a genus. A third name in italics may be added to denote a subspecies. The name of the original author of the scientific description of the species may follow the Latin name. It is enclosed in parentheses if the fish has been reclassified since the original description was published. 'Teleost' is a convenience term of historical significance, but does not at present have any validity in scientific nomenclature.

The variety of different sizes, shapes and habits of fishes is tremendous. This fact makes any generalization very difficult. The smallest known fish is a pygmy goby, found in the Philippines. It measures about 11 millimeters (half an inch) at maturity. The smallest aquarium fish is a mosquito fish, *Heterandria formosa*, which reaches a size of about ¾ inch in the male and 1½ inch in the female. The largest fishes are the whale shark (45 feet), the basking shark (40 feet) and the giant manta ray (23 feet wide). The largest specimen of the whale shark, seen but not captured (for good reason, no doubt), has been estimated at 70 feet in length and weighing 50,000 pounds.

The heaviest of the bony fishes is the ocean sunfish *(Mola mola)*; one specimen measured slightly over 10 feet and weighed 4400 pounds. Turning to freshwater fishes, the largest are the sturgeons, up to 14 feet in length and weighing 2250 pounds. Among teleosts, the largest representatives are the catfish family. The European giant catfish grows to ten feet in length and the goonch, an Indian catfish, is no slouch at six feet in length and weighing in at 250 pounds. Brazil has its *Arapaima gigas* (not a catfish) which may reach seven feet.

Population and distribution

The natural grouping of a fish species is a *population*. Its members normally interbreed and any characteristics that are genetically determined will ultimately spread through the population. Reproductive success and survival rate determine whether a population is stable, expanding or contracting. Environmental factors often determine the degree of success of a population, so that changes in temperature, salinity or oxygen content, for example, may produce typical changes in population.

Successive dominance by different populations often is found in natural waters, as conditions change gradually. One famous

The bowfin, *Amia calva*, is a remnant of a very ancient order of fishes. Photo by Dr. Herbert R. Axelrod.

One of the largest of freshwater fishes, *Arapaima gigas* (top), and one of the smallest, *Heterandria formosa* (bottom). Upper photo by Dr. Herbert R. Axelrod, lower photo by Rudolf Zukal.

Sturgeons (*Acipenser*) are the largest freshwater fishes (top), and the bulky ocean sunfish (*Mola mola*) is the heaviest of the bony fishes (bottom). Upper photo by Dr. Herbert R. Axelrod, lower photo by Wade Doak.

example is the eutrophication process of lakes, due to accumulation of more and more organic matter. It leads from dominant populations of trout, perch and pike to an ultimate preponderance of bass, sunfish and catfish and ends up with no fish population at all.

The author has seen the same evolutionary process in aquariums that were left to themselves too long. The enthusiast starts out with a mixed community tank of many beautiful species and ends up after a while with a few runty guppies and hardy catfish. One can counteract this ageing process by filtration, frequent changes of water and keeping the fish population density down; but, ultimately, nature will take its course.

Each species in a community has its own special distribution. Marine fishes, for example, may inhabit the "littoral" zone at shore, the "neritic" zone over the continental shelves or the "pelagic" zone of the open seas. Similarly, in terms of preferred depths, they may be found in the surface regions, the middle zones or the bottom. Fishes may live in the estuarine areas, where rivers enter into the ocean and where changes in salt content may be extreme as the tides move in and out. Freshwater fishes show similar specialization in distribution with the additional differentiation between lake dwellers and inhabitants of rivers and streams.

Great differences in habitat exist even within these general regions. Special situations have resulted in special adaptation, as found, for example, in the community of fishes inhabiting coral reefs or hot springs. Whole populations live in pools where temperatures as high as 108°F. are tolerated. The unique desert pupfish *(Cyprinodon)* live in water so hot it would kill any other fish.

In the home aquarium the same selection of habitat can be observed. Vertical distribution is well established, with such fishes as the hatchetfishes *(Carnegiella* or *Gasteropelecus)*, butterflyfishes *(Pantodon buchholzi)*, or killifishes occupying the

An estuary is a special environment, marked by changes in salt content of the water. Photo by Dr. Herbert R. Axelrod.

The Salt Creek pupfish, *Cyprinodon salinus*, is found only in Salt Creek, Death Valley. Due to progressive drying up of the creek there is always the threat that this species may completely disappear in the future. Photo by Dr. Martin R. Brittan.

surface; many others stay mainly in the middle regions; and bottom dwellers, such as most *Corydoras* catfishes, prefer to live in the lower regions.

The environment

Habitat selection and distribution is a function of adaptation to the environment. Fish as a whole have spread into almost every available kind of environment, although each species has tolerance for only a limited range of environmental conditions. A very complex relationship has developed between the fish and the physical characteristics of the medium in which it lives.

The environmental effects may be classified into a scale of five degrees.*

I. LETHAL CONDITIONS. Fishes are unable to sustain life. Lack of oxygen, high temperature or the presence of metallic salts would be examples.

---

* According to Fry, F. E. J. The effect of environmental factors on the physiology of fish. *In* Hoar, W. S. and Randall, D. J. (eds.) *Fish Physiology.* N.Y.: Academic Press, 1971, pp. 1–98.

II. CONTROLLING CONDITIONS. Factors that control the metabolic ·rate. Increasing temperature, for example, increases the rate of metabolism and incidentally the need for oxygen. Each species has an optimum range of temperatures and varying degrees of tolerance for fluctuations. Deep-sea dwellers have tolerance for low oxygen levels, but not much tolerance for temperature fluctuations; surface dwelling species, on the other hand, have a greater tolerance for temperature fluctuations, but need a greater oxygen concentration.

III. LIMITING CONDITIONS. Factors that restrict the choices of action open to a fish. Oxygen-poor regions, for example, would limit the areas through which a fish might travel in its search for food or block its path on migration.

IV. MASKING CONDITIONS. Effects for which the fish has a compensatory mechanism, so that the behavior will appear to be unaffected, although there

Redfin shiners (*Notropis umbratilis*) are typical freshwater "minnows." Photo by Braz Walker.

Most armored catfish like these *Corydoras* spend most of their time at the bottom of their habitat. Photo by Dr. Herbert R. Axelrod.

Many fishes of the seashore (littoral zone) hide themselves in the sand like this puffer (*Arothron* sp.). Photo by Hilmar Hansen, Aquarium Berlin.

Yellow kingfish, *Seriola grandis,* of Australia are schooling fish of the pelagic zone of the coastal and oceanic areas of Australian waters. Photo by Allan Power.

17

is a physiological price which must be paid.

V. DIRECTIVE CONDITIONS. Fishes initiate behavior that compensates for the environmental effect. These behavior patterns may involve moving into a more favorable environment, increased food intake or special mechanisms, such as going into hibernation or estivation.

For a further example, let us look at the way fishes adjust to freezing temperatures. Fishes, as mentioned earlier, belong to the so-called coldblooded animals. Unlike mammals and birds, they are unable to control their body temperature, which must rise and fall with the surrounding medium. Exceptions are found in some fast-moving fishes, like the tuna, which create a certain amount of body heat by their muscle contractions and thus keep their body temperature above that of the surrounding ocean. When the water temperature falls, the internal temperature of fishes must also decrease. Nevertheless, fishes cannot survive ice formation within their body fluids. Freshwater species move to the bottom of rivers and lakes when the surface freezes over. It happens that most bodies of water rarely freeze all the way to the bottom. Even if apparently frozen into a block of ice, fishes may be able to survive as there is likely to be a thin layer of liquid surrounding their body. Salt water can be cooled below the freezing point of water, a fact used in the old-fashioned ice cream makers and in de-icing roadways by spreading salt on them, so ocean fishes, especially in Arctic and Antarctic waters, have to protect themselves. They do so by allowing their body fluids to become super-cooled, a term applied to liquids cooled below their freezing point. Some fishes have been discovered to have glycoproteins in their bloodstream, equivalent to an anti-freeze solution like that added to a car's radiator.

Resistance to cold in tropical species, of course, cannot be directly compared with species which normally are exposed to freezing temperatures in winter. Slow acclimatization increases the chance of survival under conditions of dropping temperatures, but sharp chilling is fatal, even to cold-tolerant species. That's why aquarium heaters are so important.

Even in winter, many bodies of water remain unfrozen. Photo by Robert Gannon.

Acclimatization to heat proceeds fairly rapidly. One to three days has been found to be sufficient to increase heat resistance significantly. Even subsequent exposure to low temperature does not cause loss of this resistance to warm water. Deficiency of dissolved oxygen, rather than heat, often appears to be the limiting factor in resistance to increases in temperature. The effect of warming the environment on fish life is being extensively studied because of the danger of heat pollution, the effect of discharge of heated water into rivers or the ocean from the cooling mechanism of nuclear power plants.

Adaptation to waters of different degrees of salinity depends very much on the mechanisms available to different species for regulating their body fluids. All fishes are faced with the problem of keeping these body fluids at the appropriate degree of concentration. For freshwater fishes the tendency is for the surrounding water to enter the body cells, particularly through the gills. Though surrounded by water, they never need to drink, but do take in some water with their food. The excess fluids are excreted via the kidneys.

Marine fishes are faced with the opposite problem. They tend to lose water to the environment. To compensate they must constantly drink seawater. Obviously, they are the only fishes that "drink like a fish." Some water is also taken in with their food. Their kidneys reabsorb water, so only small, but necessary, amounts of urine are excreted. Excess salts may be excreted by special cells found in the gills and mouth region.

When placed in salt water, freshwater species can survive to the extent they can handle the increased inflow of salt. Sea water, which is a mixture of many salts, is much better tolerated than pure sodium chloride solution. It has been claimed that distilled water, which lacks all dissolved salts, is fatal to freshwater fishes. But some fishes have survived for long periods in distilled water; therefore one can speculate that it was probably the dissolved toxic contaminants from the copper tubing of the stills used, which caused the toxic reaction in water that lacked other dissolved minerals. Some marine species can acclimatize to fresh water. They stop drinking, increase urine excretion and retain body salts. Adding calcium salts to fresh water increases the ability of marine fishes to survive. Concentrations of salts above normal sea water levels prove fatal when the capacity of the gills to excrete salts is exceeded and salts are retained in body tissues.

Special situations exist in fishes that migrate between the ocean and fresh water

Although most rays live in salt water, this freshwater stingray (*Potamotrygon*) is at home in the Amazon River. Photo by Dr. Herbert R. Axelrod.

Jarbuas, *Therapon jarbua*, are equally at home in the Indian Ocean and in freshwater aquaria. Photo by Roger Steene.

The mono, *Monodactylus argenteus* (top), and the scat, *Scatophagus argus* (bottom), inhabit brackish water. Their kidneys and gills are specially adapted to changes in salinity. Photos by Dr. Herbert R. Axelrod.

or move back and forth between the two media. Young salmon develop salt-secreting cells in their gills and undergo other physiological changes before they are ready to enter the ocean from the rivers and lakes where they were born. Examples of fishes equally at home in the ocean and in fresh water are some of the monos *(Monodactylus)*, sticklebacks *(Gasterosteus)*, killifish *(Fundulus)*, mollies *(Poecilia)* and scats *(Scatophagus)*, all well-known aquarium species. Kidneys and gills of these fishes are specially adapted to compensate for the different conditions they encounter. Hormonal as well as neural control of these adjustments may be involved.

The story regarding pH tolerance of freshwater fishes is a complicated one. The term pH refers to the degree of acidity or alkalinity of the water as measured by a scale which expresses neutrality as 7.0, acidity by lower and alkalinity by higher values than 7.0. A pH range from 5.0 to 9.0 is tolerated well and more extreme values are not usually harmful, if fishes are exposed to them for short periods only.

The complications arise from the interaction of acidity and the disposal of carbon dioxide (CO_2) produced in respiration. A low pH increases the available CO_2 and reduces the ability of the blood to take up oxygen (O_2). This condition, together with increased temperature, necessitating higher respiratory rates, often proves lethal. Fishes are asphyxiated in waters that are warmed and polluted, due to this combination of factors, although pH, CO_2, and O_2 levels by themselves are within tolerable limits.

The effect of environmental factors can be understood best when their physiological basis is known. Fish behavior, in turn, must be related to the environment in which the fish spends its life.

We shall now explore the biological basis of behavior. Body function and behavior are intimately linked together and understanding of organic functioning and the anatomy of fishes is essential to understanding their behavior.

The bluehead, *Thalassoma bifasciatum*, is one of the most common inhabitants of West Indian reefs. Photo by Gerhard Marcuse.

The swim-bladder of the goldfish, *Carassius auratus*, has two gas-filled lobes of equal size. Photo by Laurence E. Perkins.

Chapter II

THE BIOLOGICAL BASIS OF BEHAVIOR

How a fish swims

Fishes must move in a three-dimensional medium; their movement may best be compared to a bird flying or to the flight of an airplane. It involves propulsion, lift and stabilization. Forward movement stems from alternating contraction of muscles on each side of the body. Eel-like fish, the kuhli loach *(Acanthophthalmus kuhlii)* for example, swim by serpentine movements of the whole body. Other fish, such as the marine dwelling trunkfish (Ostraciidae) propel themselves by movement of the tail and keep their body rigid. Most fishes, however, combine both these movements, undulations of the body and tail coordinating to provide a forward thrust. Fish can also go into reverse by reversing the thrust of their movements and stand still by just counteracting the flow of current.

You can tell a lot about the potential speed of a fish by its body shape. Elongated, torpedo-like shapes are best suited for speedy movement. (And conversely, torpedoes have a fish-like shape.) Flattened bodies indicate agility in turning, but less forward speed. Bulky fish or fish with modified tails, such as the seahorse *(Hippocampus)* move slowly, albeit often gracefully.

In most fishes the paired fins serve as stabilizers to control roll and pitch and to aid in climbing and diving, banking and turning. They also serve as brakes. The unpaired fins keep the fish on an even keel and prevent yawing.

Lift is provided by the trim of the fins and the swimbladder in fishes that come so equipped. Sharks and their relatives have no swimbladder and counteract their tendency to sink by elevating their bodies by means of the paired fins. They must keep swimming or they will sink to the bottom. Teleost species living mainly on the bottom or in tidal zones often also have no swimbladder or a modified organ that serves as a lung or a storage organ. The swimbladder can also serve both as a sound producing and a sound receiving organ (see Ch. 5).

Although swimming is the normal form of fish locomotion, it might be pointed out that some fishes are also capable of burrowing, crawling, creeping, leaping, jet propulsion and flying. Many an aquarist has lost fish by forgetting that some fishes have no qualms about leaving their watery medium, at least for short periods of time (gobies, blennies, walking catfish, mudskippers, etc.).

Skin and scales

Anyone who has eaten fish, and that includes most aquarists, knows that fish have a tough (or crisp when appropriately prepared) skin, covered in most fish with scales. The skin is an important organ; it not only provides a covering to enclose the body, but serves to regulate oxygen exchange, excretion and water pressure. In addition, it contains sense organs, nerves and bloodvessels, as well as the chromato-

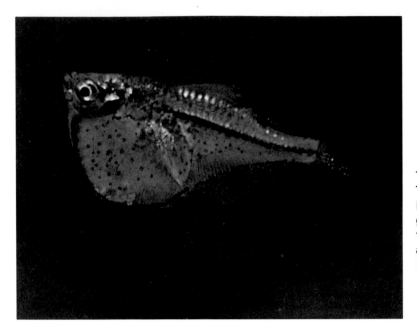

Types of swimming: The hatchetfishes (shown is a hatchetfish of the genus *Carnegiella*) are able to glide short distances above the water. Photo by Dr. Herbert R. Axelrod.

A seahorse uses its dorsal fin as an oar. Shown is *Hippocampus kuda*. Photo by Marine Studios, Marineland, Florida.

Kuhli loaches (*Acanthoph-thalmus*) move their whole body in serpentine fashion. Photo by Vojtech Elek.

The trunkfish (*Ostracion meleagris*) keeps its body rigid and propels itself by means of its tail fin. Photo by Dr. Shih-chieh Shen.

phores that give some fishes their beautiful color patterns. An important feature is the numerous mucus producing cells which secrete a slippery slime covering the body of most fishes. Anyone who has attempted to hold a struggling fish in his hand has had to contend with its ability to wriggle enough to slip through his fingers.

Scales are to fish what feathers are to birds and hair to mammals. They are an important and distinctive development in the evolution of fishes, although there are a few kinds that are naked or nearly so. Some fish have modified their scales into bony plates, such as the armored catfishes (Callichthyidae).

Sharks and rays (Chondrichthyes) have a type of scale known as placoid, which is anatomically very similar to the teeth of vertebrates. The scales have an enamel covering over a body of dentine and a pulp cavity. The scales make the skin so rough that it was used as a sandpaper substitute by old-time carpenters.

Higher bony fishes have scales made of thin, translucent bony material. usually overlapping like shingles on a roof. They may be either cycloid or ctenoid. More primitive, soft-rayed fishes tend to have the disc-like, more-or-less circular cycloid scales, while the spiny-rayed fishes usually have ctenoid scales, bearing comb-like spiny processes on their posterior margin, the part which is buried in the skin. Exceptions occur in many popular aquarium fishes, such as characins, killifish, anabantoids and livebearers (Poeciliidae), which have ctenoid scales, although they are soft-rayed.

Scales are of much use to the ichthyologist in identification. Often a single scale is enough to classify a fish, at least as far as the family to which it belongs. Scale counts are another aid that has proven highly useful in taxonomy.

The scales of many species may be used to estimate the age of a fish. Growth rings, like those found in trees, are laid down annually, as the fish grows and the scales

Placoid scale

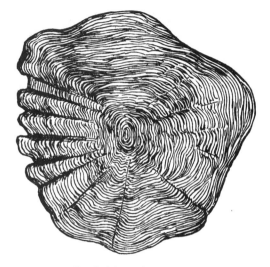

Cycloid scale

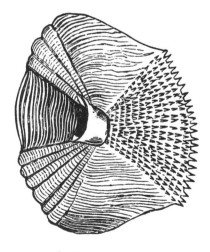

Ctenoid scale

Three types of scales.

Head of the venomous stonefish *Synanceja verrucosa* showing extreme modification of the skin. Its venom is carried in thirteen spines along its back. Photo by Gerhard Marcuse.

grow with it. They can tell the story of a fish life. A 10 millimeter scale of an Atlantic salmon can give evidence of the four years it spent in a river growing up, a year at sea, an ascent up a river to spawn, a further year at sea and part of a fourth year, when it was caught attempting to enter a river for a second spawning. Disease, injury, starvation, pollution and any other unfavorable condition leave their mark and form a record for the knowledgeable reader.

The beautiful colors of many fishes also originate in the skin. Iridescent colors depend on physical refraction of light, giving rise to interference colors which are reflected back to the viewer from underlying dark pigments. The silvery color that is so commonly found in fishes is due to a reflection of incident light by crystal-line guanin, a waste product of metabolism. It is extracted from fish scales commercially and used as a pigment in such products as pearlite nailpolish.

True pigment colors are contained in chromatophores, embedded in the skin either outside or beneath the scales. The pigment granules may disperse throughout the cell or concentrate in the center, thus accounting for the color changes often seen in fish. Pigments appear colored because they selectively absorb or reflect certain wavelengths of incident light. Commonly found pigments are the flavins (yellow and fluorescent), pterins (white, yellow, red and orange), melanins (black and brown), carotenoids (yellow, orange and red) and purines (white or silvery).

Color changes play a role as signals in fish behavior, and they may be used for

Silvery scales provide the cool shine of *Tetragonopterus argenteus* (left) and, in exaggerated form, of the pearlscale oranda, *Carassius auratus* (bottom). Left photo by Dr. Herbert R. Axelrod, bottom photo by Kosmos Verlag.

Iridescent flashes mark the sparkling appearance of the cardinal tetra, *Cheirodon axelrodi*. Photo by Stanislav Frank.

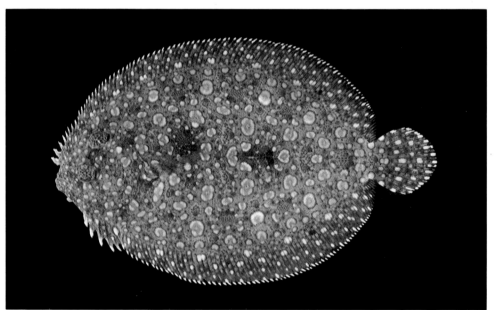

The pigmentation of the tropical flounder *Bothus mancus* is subject to change depending on its background. Photo by Dr. John E. Randall.

Melanin is the pigment responsible for the black color of this black lyretail molly, *Poecilia latipinna*.

Pterois volitans, like all of the other zebrafishes (also called turkeyfishes and lionfishes), possesses venomous spines. Photo by Wilhelm Hoppe.

concealment and camouflage. Two modes of control of these changes have been discovered. Hormonal influences are centered in the pituitary, which secretes hormones that are generally concerned with color intensification. The adrenals pour out epinephrine, which has the effect of aggregating the melanophores and thus causes the fish to go pale. This is a typical fright response. The second mode is nervous control. Two antagonistic sets of nerve endings terminate on the chromatophores. Activity of one set produces color intensification; activity of the antagonist causes lightening of colors.

The eyes are of primary importance as the receptors most concerned with initiating color changes. Blinded fishes generally do not respond to the shading, color or pattern of their environment. They usually turn dark and remain so regardless of illumination. However, extra-optic reception also may play a role. The pineal complex and direct illumination of the skin, for example, are additional sources of pigmentation control.

A very curious and not uncommon attribute of many deep-sea and bottom-dwelling fishes is the *production* of light. This bioluminescence may be due to photophores, light producing cells embedded in the skin, with a reflector layer and a lens-like covering. These cells appear to be under direct nervous control. A second type of luminescence is due to the presence of symbiotic luminous bacteria. These live in special pockets, supplied with an excellent bloodvessel complex. Since the output of their light is continuous, special mechanisms have evolved to turn the light on and off. For example, *Photoblepharon palpebratus* and *Anomalops katoptron* are indigenous to the Banda Sea in eastern Indonesia. Both species show spectacular flashes of light from a pair of suborbital elliptical organs. *Anomalops* extinguishes its light by turning its hinged organ downward into a black-pigmented pocket; *Photoblepharon* has a black fold which can be drawn over its organ like an eyelid. *Anomalops* is a shallow-water species and its light organs, situated below the eye, may be extended 180° to the body.

It might be mentioned in passing that venom glands are also derived from skin tissue. They are presumed to be modified mucus glands. Stings from venomous fishes are painful, to say the least, and may be lethal. Saltwater aquarium enthusiasts will be familiar with the beautiful but very poisonous scorpionfishes (Scorpaenidae), toadfishes, and the like.

A slightly frightened angelfish, *Pterophyllum scalare*. The vertical bars on its side have gone pale, compared to the intense black bars on the angelfish on page 6. Photo by James Dunbar.

Anomalops katoptron displays a large light organ below the eye. Photo by Dr. Herbert R. Axelrod.

Gonostoma elongatum has an array of variably sized light organs along the side of the body. Photo by Paul Allen.

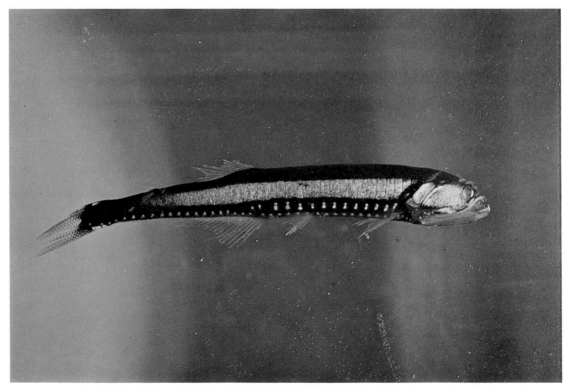

Siamese fighting fish, *Betta splendens*, have been specially bred for color. They often come to the surface to take a gulp of air. Photo by Dr. Herbert R. Axelrod.

Tilapia "digging" a hole, preliminary to spawning, by expelling a jet of water. Photo by Chvojka Milan.

Breathing

The difficulty for most mammals and vertebrates with breathing underwater is the greater density of the water and the lower levels of dissolved oxygen, as compared to air. Fishes had evolved an efficient system of extracting the available oxygen by means of their gills, and, in addition, a number of species had developed the capacity of utilizing atmospheric oxygen.

Neglecting the different arrangements found in the various classes of fishes, the common problem is solved by circulating water over thinly walled surfaces in the gills, which contain a vast network of fine bloodvessels. In the teleosts a pump is employed by which water enters the mouth, is forced through the gills and expelled through the gill cover, the operculum. Oxygen diffuses into the bloodvessels and carbon dioxide is given off as the water circulates through the gills. Breathing rate

depends on many factors, such as temperature, oxygen concentration and movement of the fish. Swiftly swimming fishes tend to utilize the flow of water, leaving their mouth and gill flaps open as they swim to aid their breathing. Slow swimming and sedentary fishes have larger gill cavities and deeper breathing movements. The breathing process is very efficient, utilizing 50 to 80 per cent of available oxygen.

Fishes also have a coughing or sneezing reflex, by which the flow of water may occasionally be reversed to dislodge small particles of dirt from the gill surfaces and to blow them out through the mouth or gill openings. The pump can be reversed to expel a jet of water from the mouth, a movement often seen when fishes are cleaning a rock or slate preparatory to spawning or "digging" a hole in the bottom sand of an aquarium.

For various reasons fishes may have to supplement their underwater respiration by breathing air. Many tropical fishes live in water that has a low oxygen content or dries up, forcing the fishes to move across land to survive. Gills are not well adapted to air breathing, as they need water to support their fine structure and collapse in air, due to lack of stiffeners, so few fishes rely on gills for air breathing.

Various different adaptations have evolved. Special modified skin folds in the lining of the pharynx or gill chambers serve as accessory air breathing organs in a number of cases. Best known to aquarists is the labyrinthine organ of anabantoids such as *Betta*, *Macropodus* and the gouramis. These fishes have become so dependent on their accessory breathing organs that they will drown if they cannot reach the water surface at regular intervals. Other fishes using similar means are catfishes of the genera *Clarias* and *Saccobranchus*, and the snakeheads (*Ophicephalus*). The little mudskippers (*Periophthalmus*) have become so well adapted to life out of the water that they seek their food on land and may often be found climbing around on the roots of mangrove trees in a most unfishlike manner, in their search for insects to eat.

Another kind of adaptation is found in the air swallowers. Many armored catfish such as *Corydoras, Callichthys, Plecostomus* and *Loricaria* have a thin-walled stomach, serving as a respiratory organ. The loaches (Cobitidae) have an intestine that serves alternately for digestion and respiration. The weatherfish *(Cobitis taenia)* presumably gets its weather forecasting ability from the sensitivity to changes in barometric pressure in this swallowed air.

The swim bladder serves as an accessory air breathing organ in the bowfin *(Amia calva)*, a rather primitive, but very successfully adapted swamp dweller. An even more primitive fish, the African bichir or reedfish *(Polypterus)*, has a well-developed laterally bilobed gas bladder serving the adult as a respiratory organ. Other oc-

casional air breathers using the swim bladder as accessory organs range from the giant South American *Arapaima* to the African elephant-nosed mormyrids (Mormyridae) and their relative, the African knife fish *Gymnarchus*.

Fishes can have lungs! Once abundant, the three kinds of lungfishes that are found today are practically unchanged from their ancestors which inhabited a quite different earth some 300 million years ago. The three genera, the Australian lungfish *(Neoceratodus)*, the African lungfish *(Protopterus)* and the South Amercian lungfish *(Lepidosiren)* possess gills as well as fully developed lungs. Their gills are inefficient and they must have access to atmospheric air. The African and the South American lungfishes live in waters that dry up during part of the year. During the dry season they live in burrows which they dig in preparation for their summer rest or estivation.

Modifications of the gills into a labyrinthine organ in anabantoids.

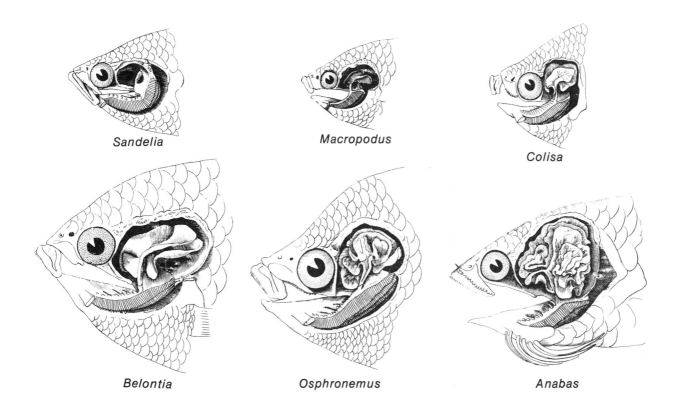

Sandelia

Macropodus

Colisa

Belontia

Osphronemus

Anabas

Magnified view of a portion of the gill of a trout. In this illustration there has been some damage to the gill filaments.

Cross-section (magnified) through the gill filament of a whitefish (*Chondrostoma*).

The red snakehead, *Ophicephalus micropeltes* (top), and the mudskipper (*Periophthalmus*) (bottom) rely on their accessory breathing organs when out of the water. Upper photo by Dr. D. Terver, Nancy Aquarium, bottom photo by Hilmar Hansen, Aquarium Berlin.

The weatherfish *Cobitis taenia* swallows air which it can absorb through its digestive tract. Weatherfish are said to predict changes in the weather by their restlessness preceding a storm. It may well be that changes in barometric pressure associated with stormy weather make them feel uncomfortable. Photo by Chvojka Milan.

When the rainy season again floods their burrows, they wake up from their sleep-like state and return to the watery life of a fish. The Australian lungfish is not known to burrow or estivate.

Reports are often received of eels *(Anguilla anguilla)* crawling across damp meadows on migration. They are capable of moving on land, because their skin can serve as a respiratory organ. Cutaneous respiration is sufficient for eels, as long as the temperature is below 60°F., a fact which may explain why eels mainly migrate overland at night.

Circulation

Oxygen extracted from the surrounding medium and carbon dioxide produced by the fish metabolism, as well as nutrients and waste products are carried through the body by the circulatory system. With the possible exception of the lungfishes, it is a single circulation in which the heart pumps deoxygenated blood to the gills, where it is aerated and the carbon dioxide given off. The oxygenated blood is then distributed by the arteries to the body tissues and then returned to the heart via the veins. The lungfishes, some reptiles and all birds and mammals have a more efficient double system in which the heart pumps both oxygenated and deoxygenated blood in two separate closed circuits to the body and lungs respectively.

Fish have low blood pressure and relatively small, slow beating hearts. Their blood volume is also relatively low. With the exception of the Antarctic icefishes (Chaenichthyidae), their blood is red, due to its hemoglobin content. The Antarctic icefishes lack red blood corpuscles and carry their respiratory gases in their colorless blood plasma. Fish blood clots faster than that of other vertebrates. The reason for this fact is not yet known, and is indeed somewhat of a mystery, as fish blood is low in the clotting factor pro-thrombin, but no doubt it comes in handy for injured fish, whose bleeding would tend to attract enemies.

Collecting and digesting food

Fish feed on a very wide variety of foods and have evolved many specialized feeding patterns and variations of the digestive mechanisms to deal with their food. The behavioral aspects of feeding will be discussed later. Major types of feeding adaptation are the food strainers, the

The South American lungfish *Lepidosiren paradoxus* (top) and the Australian lungfish *Neoceratodus fosteri* (bottom) are living fossils. Top photo by Harald Schultz, bottom photo by Gerhard Budich.

The bichir *Polypterus bichir* belongs to a very ancient order of fishes in which the gas bladder is used as a respiratory organ. Photo by Klaus Paysan.

Eels (*Anguilla*) often move overland on their migrations. Their skin serves as an accessory breathing organ. Photo by Dr. D. Terver, Nancy Aquarium.

The African lungfish *Protopterus annectens* must breathe air to survive; deprived of access to the surface, the lungfish would drown. Photo by Dr. Herbert R. Axelrod.

The bonytongues (Osteoglossidae), including the arowana, *Osteoglossum bicirrhosum*, and its close relative *Scleropages formosus* (illustrated), as well as the giant arapaima (p. 12), are able to live a long time out of water because of their accessory breathing organs. Photo by Kenneth M. Bertin.

Kissing gouramis, *Helostoma temmincki*, use their enlarged lips in social behavior as well as when feeding. Photo by G.J.M. Timmerman.

The bristly-mouthed tetra, *Tyttocharax madeirae*, has teeth spilling over on to the lips and snout.

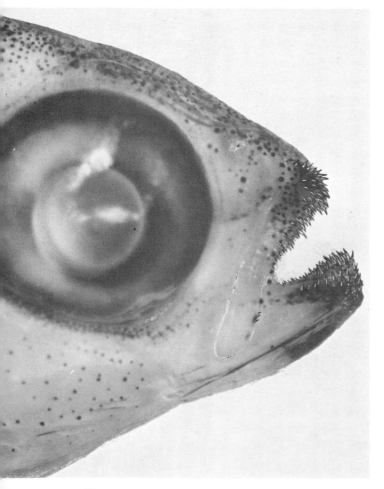

grazers, the suckers and the predators. Food straining consists of taking a more or less indiscriminate mouthful of food organisms and water, straining this "soup" through a sieve-like mechanism, and expelling the water while retaining the food. The sieve usually consists of specially enlarged gill rakers, comb-like processes on the inside of the gill arches. Some of the largest fish, the whale shark *(Rhincodon)* and the basking shark *(Cetorhinus)* are food strainers. A variation of this theme is represented by the mud strainers, which root through the bottom debris and filter out food particles. *Geophagus* and many Malawian cichlids are good examples.

Grazers take little bites of food, thoroughly browsing over a feeding area before moving on to the next. This mode of feeding may involve plant material (herbivores), small animal life (carnivores) or both (omnivores). Specialized grazers search the water surface, coral reefs, even the bodies of other fish.

Fishes with enlarged lips are likely to use a sucking mode of feeding. Instead of biting off their food, they employ a sucking movement to ingest food particles. These fishes often root in the bottom sediment. They may spit out inedible particles or swallow mud and edible content indiscriminately and let their digestive system take care of sorting out the mixture.

Predatory feeders are fishes with big mouths and sharp teeth that feed on other animals. They may hunt by stealth, like a cat, lying in wait for their victims, or chase them by means of their superior speed and agility, like a wolf. Some hunt by sight, whereas others rely on their sense of smell to locate their prey. The anglerfishes (Lophiidae and Antennariidae) are among the fishes that have developed a special lure to attract their victims. The archer fish *(Toxotes jaculator)* shoots down insects with a spray of water. Most predatory fishes swallow their prey whole and have a mouthful of sharp teeth to prevent the escape of their catch. Piranha *(Serrasalmus)* and many sharks, however, take bites out of larger prey.

The shapes of the mouth and lips have undergone many kinds of modification in response to special feeding habits. Most general is a thin-lipped mouth with hinged jaws that allow the mouth to open wide. Many fish will use the inrush of water, when the mouth is opened, as a means of ingesting small crustaceans, such as *Daphnia*, or tiny fishes. Mouthbreeders utilize the same movement to recapture their young, after they have gone for a "walk." An exaggerated version of this method of feeding is found in the leaf fish *(Monocirrhus polyacanthus)*, whose mouth is extra huge and seems to unfold into a tube-like snout when unsuspecting small fishes pass by the apparently drifting leaf these fishes resemble.

Enlarged lips are very prominent in kissing gouramis *(Helostoma)*, where they play a role in social behavior, as well as in feeding. Suctorial discs in the armored South American loricariid catfishes, such as *Plecostomus*, serve not only for cleaning off algae from plants and rocks, but are also used as holdfasts when the fish are at rest in swift flowing streams. The jawless (Agnatha) lampreys and hagfishes are the vampires of the fish world. They have suctorial mouths by which they attach themselves to other fish while rasping a hole in their victim's side in order to feed on their blood.

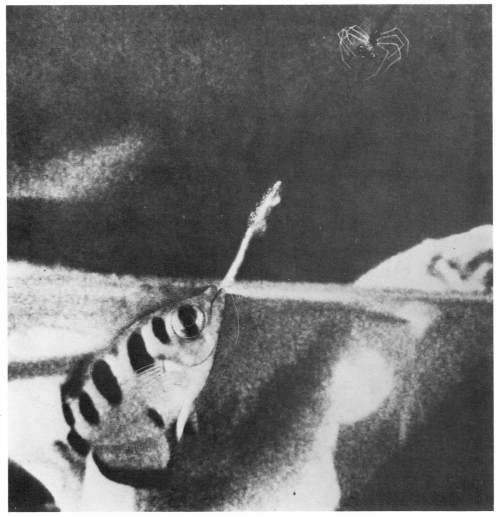

The archer fish *Toxotes jaculator* has a unique method of feeding. It presses its tongue against a groove in the roof of its mouth to form a tube through which it aims a stream of water at insect targets above the water surface. New York Zoological Society photo.

The South American leaf fish, *Monocirrhus polyacanthus*, resembles a drifting leaf until some food comes into view, when it unfolds its huge snout and engulfs its prey. Photo by Hans Joachim Richter.

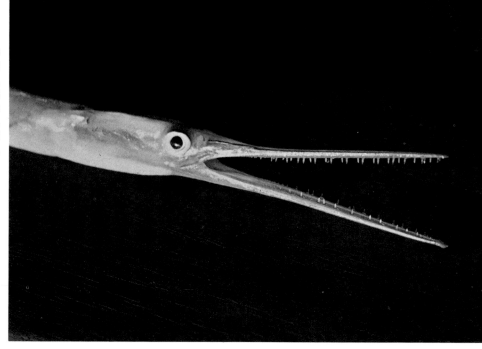

Needlefishes (*Strongylura*) are not only needle-shaped, but their mouth is also filled with needle-sharp teeth. Photo by Dr. Herbert R. Axelrod.

The longnosed filefish, *Oxymonacanthus longirostris*, uses its elongated snout to pick out the polyps of living coral, its principal natural food. Photo by Dr. Herbert R. Axelrod.

Moray eels like this *Muraena helena* have sharp teeth and bad temper—a dangerous combination. Photo by Miloslav Kocar.

Extreme specialization is found in the halfbeaks (Hemiramphidae), for example the Malayan halfbeak *(Dermogenys pusillus)*, whose lower jaw is greatly enlarged in an apparent adaptation to surface feeding. Forceps-like beaks that can reach into all kinds of nooks and crannies of coral reefs are found in the beautiful marine butterfly fishes (Chaetodontidae). The seahorses and pipefishes (Syngnathidae) and their relatives have their jaws modified into a fused tube through which food is sucked as through a straw.

Most peculiar proboscid snouts are found in certain South American fishes and some of the African mormyrids, such as the appendage of the appropriately named elephant-nosed fish *(Gnathonemus)*. In fact, the whole mormyrid group shows a tendency to individualized modification of the usual fish "face." Moreover, this group is also weakly electric.

Teeth arose first in the fishes and the placoid scales of sharks still grade over into teeth as they progress from skin covering to jaws and mouth cavity. In bony fishes, teeth may be found almost anywhere in the mouth. They are located not only on the jaws, but also on the roof of the mouth, the tongue and the sides of the throat, where so-called pharyngeal teeth grow from various elements of the gill arches. The tiny bristly-mouthed tetra, *Tyttocharax madeirae*, even has some spilling over on the lips and snout.

Depending on the diet, teeth are modified to best serve their purpose. As mentioned above, predatory fish tend to swallow their prey whole, the function of the teeth being to hold on to their prey, not to chew. Their teeth accordingly curve backward, so that once a victim is impaled, it hardly ever has a chance to go any way but down the throat. Moray eels (Muraenidae) and some other fishes have canine-like teeth which fold backward to let food pass, then snap back into a locked position. Crushing and grinding type teeth are found in fishes that feed on snails, clams and hard-shelled crustaceans. Razor-sharp cutting teeth adorn the mouth of piranhas *(Serrasalmus)* and barracuda *(Sphyraena)*. Grazers often have scissor-like, sharply edged cutting teeth, such as the parrot-like beak of the parrotfishes (Scaridae). Food strainers may have no teeth, a condition also true for other specialized feeders, as for example the seahorses *(Hippocampus)*.

The location of the teeth corresponds only roughly to their function. While cutting and holding teeth tend to be placed in the front of the mouth and grinding teeth in the throat, there are many exceptions. As an example, one might cite three groups of herbivorous fishes, the surgeonfish *(Acanthurus)*, the carp *(Cyprinus)* and the mullet *(Mugil)*. The first employs teeth placed in the mouth, the second grinds its food by means of pharyngeal teeth, while the third does not use teeth at all, but grinds its food in the stomach, which has been modified into a gizzard.

Food on its way down the throat passes the gill rakers, projecting from the inside of the gill arches. In their simplest form these merely protect the tender tissues of the gills. The gill rakers may bear small teeth, to prevent escape of live food. The most highly developed gill rakers are found in the food strainers, where they assist in sorting out small edible animals (plankton) from the surrounding water, which is then expelled through the gill openings. Feathery structures have developed in the flounders (Pleuronectidae), where their overlapping branches form a fine sieve.

The esophagus connects the throat to

Marine butterflyfishes, such as this longnosed butterflyfish or forcepsfish, *Forcipiger flavissimus,* are well adapted to extract food from coral reef crevices. Photo by Gerhard Marcuse.

The tasseled wobbegong, *Orectolobus ogilby*, feeds mainly on mollusks and crustaceans. Numerous tentacles around mouth make it more sensitive to its prey. Photo by Roger Steene.

In the scarlet frogfish or anglerfish, *Antennarius nummifer*, a flap of skin dangling above the fish's mouth serves as a lure to attract small fishes into feeding range. Photo by Dr. John E. Randall.

A bottom-digging African cichlid (*Haplochromis* sp.) at work searching for food or preparing a spawning site. Photo by Hilmar Hansen, Aquarium Berlin.

The fleshy lips of this Malawian cichlid, *Melanochromis labrosus*, are apparently used for searching for food. Photo by Dr. Herbert R. Axelrod.

A sharp beak-like modification of the teeth allows the parrotfishes, such as this surf parrotfish, *Scarus fasciatus*, to graze on bits of coral reef. Photo by Allan Power.

the stomach. It is distensible, so large food can pass down easily. Fishes rarely choke, but some fishes, catfishes and sticklebacks for example, if swallowed, can bring a lot of grief to a predator with their erectile spines, which cause them to become lodged in the esophagus. The author has seen a clawed frog *(Xenopus)* choke to death on a *Corydoras* catfish it had greedily swallowed. The spines had penetrated the sides of the throat. An emergency operation was performed, but it was too late to help either the fish or the frog.

Another observation concerns fish fry. Baby fishes always grow at unequal rates and inevitably the larger ones make a meal out of their smaller brothers and sisters. The author has frequently seen fishes in trouble and choking to death, when they tried to swallow another baby of just about the same size as themselves. On the other hand, deep-sea swallowers (Saccopharyngidae) have distensible jaws, esophagus and a stomach adapted to swallowing fishes that are larger than themselves under normal circumstances.

You can tell a lot about a fish by its stomach. Not only is the stomach content of a freshly caught fish an excellent indication of its feeding habits, but the nature of the stomach itself can tell a tale. Elongated stomachs are typical of predatory fishes; curved sac-like structures mark the specialized omnivore. A special feature of fishes is one or many blind tubes running from the stomach, the so-called caeca, found, for example, in the stomach of the perch *(Perca)*.

Many modifications of the basic plan exist. Already mentioned has been the gizzard-like grinding stomach, more typical of birds than fishes, that is found not only in mullet *(Mugil)*, but also in sturgeon *(Acipenser)* and gizzard shad *(Dorosoma)*. Puffers (Tetraodontidae) and porcupine-fishes (Diodontidae) have the ability to inflate themselves by filling their stomach with water or air until they resemble nothing so much as a spiky, round ball. A considerable number of species have dis-

pensed with the stomach altogether, the esophagus terminating directly into the intestine. This condition is found in herbivores, carnivores and plankton feeders, for example the roach *(Rutilus)*, the saurie *(Scomberesox)* and the seahorse *(Hippocampus)*.

The length of the intestine varies with the diet of the fish. Carnivorous teleosts tend to have intestines of one-third to three-quarters of the body length, while plant and mud feeders have intestines from two to five times their length, with extremes reaching up to fifteen times. Short intestines are found, for example, in the pike *(Esox)*, while long, coiled intestines are typical of the armored catfishes (Loricariidae). From one to over a thousand caeca may be present. In the sturgeon *(Acipenser)* these are fused together into a compact gland-like organ. The intestine itself is digested and absorbed in a number of fishes that undertake a migration to their breeding ground on maturity for spawning and die after they have fulfilled their destiny. Examples are the lamprey *(Petromyzon marinus)*, the Pacific salmon *(Oncorhynchus)* and the eel *(Anguilla anguilla)*.

Close-up of the suckermouth of the bushy-mouthed catfish *Xenocara dolichoptera*. Photo by Harald Schultz.

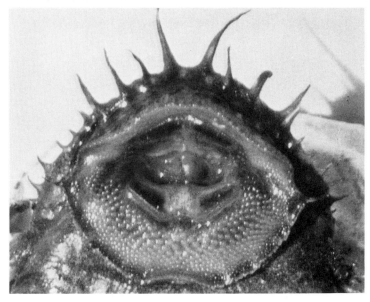

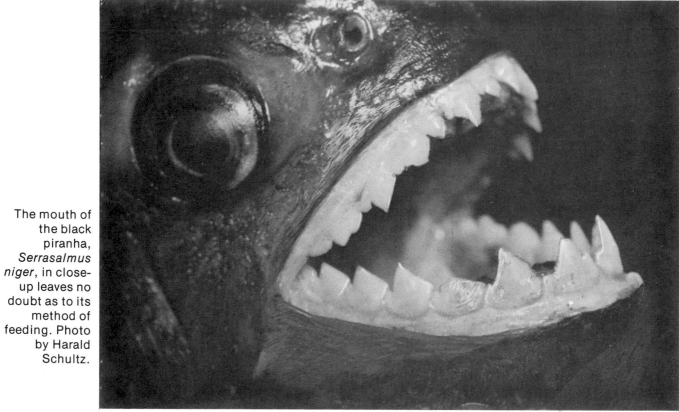

The mouth of the black piranha, *Serrasalmus niger*, in close-up leaves no doubt as to its method of feeding. Photo by Harald Schultz.

The mouth of this livebearing Malayan halfbeak, *Dermogenys pusillus*, is well adapted to surface feeding. Photo by Rudolf Zukal.

Many predatory fishes, such as this agujeta, *Boulengerella maculata* from the Amazon, have a pike-like shape. Photo by Dr. Herbert R. Axelrod.

The African tigerfish *Hydrocinus goliath* can inflict a nasty bite. Photo by Dr. J.P. Gosse.

The mormyrid *Gnathonemus curvirostris* has an elephant-like proboscis. Photo by Klaus Paysan.

The payara, *Hydrolicus scomberoides*, from Rio Negro, Venezuela sports a sharp set of teeth. Photo by Dr. Herbert R. Axelrod.

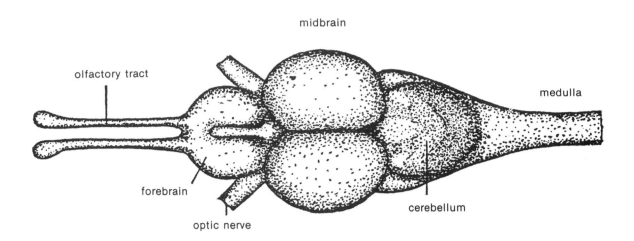

midbrain

olfactory tract

medulla

forebrain

cerebellum

optic nerve

Top view of fish brain.

Excretion

The elimination of body waste products and the maintenance of the water-salt balance are the main functions of the kidneys. They are paired, reddish-brown, extended structures lying just below the backbone. They contain a complex system of tubules and ducts designed to filter and absorb various fluids.

Freshwater fishes and marine fishes face essentially opposing problems. The kidneys of freshwater fishes must dispose of water that is constantly entering their bodies. They must also dispose of small amounts of nitrogenous waste products and retain salts. They tend to have large kidneys, passing a great amount of water. Some of the salts are reabsorbed in the kidneys, others are ingested with food and absorbed by the gills.

Marine fishes constantly lose water to their environment. The seawater they drink replaces their water loss, but the extra salt presents a problem. They rid themselves of this surplus by excreting salts through their gills. It might be noted that marine cyclostomes (Myxinidae) and sharks maintain their blood at a salt concentration that matches that of seawater, so they neither have to drink nor excrete excess salts.

The nervous system

The nervous system is the control center for behavior. It carries information from the sense organs to centralized storage and switching circuits and sends out commands to activate the muscles and glands that determine what a fish will do next. It is made up of a very large number of specialized cells, the neurons, which can be stimulated to trigger an electro-chemical discharge which travels down the length of the neuron and under appropriate conditions is chemically propagated across a tiny gap, known as the synapse, separating one neuron from another and from muscle cells. The message a neuron carries is coded as a pattern of electrical pulses, comparable to the frequency modulation (FM) system of radio transmission. Facilitation or inhibition at the synapse determines the direction the message will take or whether it will be passed along altogether. Priorities depend on the strength of the signal, the availability of pathways and whether the message is coming over the mainline or a branchline.

Neurons are bundled together into nerves which terminate in complexes known as centers or nuclei. Much can be learned by recording the pattern of incoming signals or by extirpating some of the structures and studying the subsequent loss of function, if any.

The nervous system of fishes, although less complicated than that of more highly evolved vertebrates, shows the same general plan and is analogous in most respects to that of man. As in the human nervous system, there are three major divisions, the autonomic nervous system, the peripheral nervous system and the central nervous system.

The autonomic nervous system mediates functions which do not demand a direct centralized control. These include the digestive actions of the stomach and intestine, the control of heart beat and blood pressure and the contraction of the iris of the eye, for example. Typical for fishes alone is the control of secretion of gases into the swimbladder.

The peripheral nerves carry incoming impulses from the sense organs, the skin and the interior of the body to the spinal cord and brain. They also transmit outgoing messages to the muscles to initiate contraction and relaxation in locomotion, breathing and body orientation. Depending on their point of origin, they are the spinal nerves, extending from the spinal cord, or the cranial nerves, arising directly from the brain.

The central nervous system consists of the spinal cord and the brain. The spinal cord carries ascending and descending fiber bundles from the body to the brain and from the brain to the body. A pair of spinal nerves arises from each vertebra and innervates a specific segment of skin and muscles. The spinal cord plays an important role in addition to serving as a connecting link. For example, by itself and in conjunction with higher centers it controls swimming motions. These movements are part of the reflex organization of behavior and are typical of the kind of pre-programmed behavior segments maintained by reflex action.

The spinal cord becomes the medulla where it enters the skull. Most of the cranial nerves originate here. It is a relay center, where incoming messages are collected and sent on. Swimming and other body

Tilapia mariae with young. Parental behavior is disturbed by interference with forebrain function. Photo by Gerhard Marcuse.

Pike cichlid (*Crenicichla lepidota*) swallowing a cichlid, possibly a blue acara, *Aequidens pulcher.* Photo by Dr. Herbert R. Axelrod.

A parrotfish-like wrasse (*Pseudodax moluccanus*) bares its teeth to be picked by an approaching cleaner wrasse (*Labroides dimidiatus*). Photo by Allan Power.

Triggerfishes (*Abalistes* species is shown in closeup) are best known for a spiny dorsal fin that the fish can lock into an erect position. Their teeth are well adapted to picking food out of coral reef crevices. Photo by Dr. Herbert R. Axelrod.

Lake Malawi cichlids grazing on algae. Photo by Dr. Herbert R. Axelrod.

Freshwater hatchetfishes jump out of the water when startled. The species shown is *Gasteropelecus stern-icla.* Photo by Rudolf Zukal.

movements, such as the rhythm of the fin beat are regulated by the medulla. The control of breathing, equilibrium, salt balance and skin color are among its other functions.

A pair of giant neurons, the Mauthner cells, are found in the medulla of teleosts. When a single Mauthner cell is stimulated by an electric pulse, a characteristic flip of the tail is produced. There is also a sudden movement of the eyeballs and the gill covers. The whole pattern resembles the startled response of a fish when the light is suddenly turned on in a fish tank or someone foolishly knocks on the glass of an aquarium. Interestingly, when both neurons are excited simultaneously, the tail slap is inhibited completely, while the

other components of the response remain unchanged. The purpose of the Mauthner cells seems to be to initiate a quick reflex movement to get out of the way of a predator, such as a bird, swooping down to catch itself a fish dinner with its beak and claws. The inhibition may be concerned with preventing an immediate reactivation of a tail flip, before the peak response has passed. The Mauthner cells work somewhat differently in various species. In the hatchetfishes *(Gasteropelecus),* for example, the reflex response is modified, so that these fishes jump out of the water, when startled.

The cerebellum lies in front of the medulla and where it is well developed, as in some sharks and advanced bony fishes, it forms a highly convoluted lobe, covering much of the brain. It is particularly large in the mormyrids (Mormyridae) and among catfishes (Siluroidei). Its loss is marked by disequilibrium and disturbances in coordinated swimming movements. The cerebellum is considered to be the location of fine adjustment of muscle contractions and maintenance of posture. In the mormyrids it may also be concerned with the control of their electrical activity.

The midbrain of fishes has a pair of large lobes, known as the optic lobes, as its most prominent structure. The optic nerves, carrying impulses from the eyes, end in the optic lobes. Fibers from the right eye run to the left lobe, while fibers from the left eye run to the right lobe. Vision, but not all light reception, is mediated by the optic lobes. Deeper regions of the midbrain are concerned with eye-muscle coordination.

In front of the midbrain and partially covered by it, are a number of important brain structures. These include the pineal organ just below the skull. The thalamus and hypothalamus are found in the deeper regions and the hypophysis or pituitary gland is located on the ventral part, where it is attached by a stalk to the floor of the brain. The pineal organ is a light receptor, which forms a well-developed third eye in the Agnatha; it retains some sensory function in higher fishes as well. The thalamus is concerned with sensory integration, receiving many fibers from the olfactory tract and the optic nerve. The hypothalamus and pituitary are concerned with the regulation of body functions, particularly those under control of the autonomic nervous system and the endocrine glands.

The most anterior region of the fish brain is made up of the forebrain. It receives impulses from the olfactory nerves terminating in the olfactory bulbs. The large lobes found in the forebrain were frequently called olfactory lobes, as smell was the only function attributed to them. A number of recent studies have indicated, however, that many higher coordinating and integrating functions may be attributed to these lobes, so they are now called cerebral hemispheres to indicate their relationship to the cerebral cortex in mammals, which is the part of the brain that is so prominent, if you look at a picture of a human brain, for example.

Injury to the forebrain alters normal aggressive behavior in such fishes as the jewel fish *(Hemichromis bimaculatus)* and the Siamese fighting fish *(Betta splendens)*. They show less fighting in social situations that normally induce aggression, but when it does occur, it is as vigorous as ever. Various aspects of parental and reproductive behavior are also disturbed by interference with the forebrain of such species as the African mouthbreeder *(Tilapia macrocephala)*, the platy species *(Xiphophorus maculatus)* and the three-spined stickleback *(Gasterosteus aculeatus)*.

The effect of injuries to the forebrain on learning is very interesting. Rather than total loss of learned response that might have been expected, fishes show a relative decline in behavior they had previously learned to do consistently and rapidly. These various effects have been interpreted as due to two different forebrain functions. One is the specific location of certain behavior patterns, the second is a general, non-specific arousal. Arousal is defined as the ability to respond to new situations, to initiate complex patterns of behavior and to suppress irrelevant stimulation. This hypothesis also fits in well with the non-specific activating function that has been detected in the so-called limbic system in mammals. The limbic system significantly involves the structures of the old "smell" brain (rhinencephalon) of mammals, of which the forebrain of fishes is the precursor.

Sex and reproduction

Fish as a rule possess either male or female sex organs, although some instances of hermaphroditism and at least

A mouthbrooder, *Hemihaplochromis philander,* carrying her eggs. Photo by Rudolf Zukal.

Siamese fighting fish, *Betta splendens*. Injury to the forebrain alters this species' normal aggressive behavior, but when fighting does occur it is as as vigorous as ever. Photo by Dr. Herbert R. Axelrod.

one case of parthenogenesis are known. The sex organs of the male are the testes. These paired structures are carried in the upper body cavity, alongside the swimbladder, when it is present. Spermatozoa develop in the testes and when ripe are passed down the sperm ducts, where they are activated by secretions and made ready to leave the body.

The paired ovaries of the female lie just below the swimbladder, but are often fused and shortened. Eggs pass down the oviduct where a shell is secreted around them and discharged when mature. Livebearing fishes, such as the guppy, employ internal fertilization and the development of the eggs takes place in the ovary. In many livebearing sharks, however, the eggs develop in a modified oviduct, which may then be considered the equivalent of an uterus. A few sharks, for example the dogfish *(Mustelis canis)*, have developed a true placenta, in which they nourish their embryos directly via folds in the uterus for the ten months gestation period.

In many of the livebearing topminnows such as platies, mollies and swordtails (Poeciliidae) the covering of the ovaries serves as a retaining layer for live spermatozoa, which may be stored there for as long as ten months. Thus one fertilization is sufficient for a number of broods. Superfetation, the development of several broods simultaneously but with each at a different stage of development, occurs in a number of livebearers, for example in *Heterandria formosa*.

Functional hermaphrodites exist among the sea basses (Serranidae) and porgies (Sparidae). In some species of these two families the gonads show distinct testicular and ovarian zones; in other words, both male and female functions occur in the same organ. Hermaphrodites belonging to the order Iniomi, such as *Omosudis lowei* and *Alepisaurus ferox*, on the other hand, have the testicular part of their gonads well separated from the ovarian region.

The apparent sex reversal of swordtails *(Xiphophorus helleri)* with age has often been observed. It looks as if mature females turn into males, as their anal fins become elongated and resemble the male's intromittent organ, the gonopodium. This reversal seems to be non-functional, however, and affects outward appearance only.

The case for parthenogenesis rests on the example of *Poecilia (=Mollienisia) formosa*. This fish was originally thought to be a separate species of mollie, but females only, no males, were ever collected. The scientific mystery was solved, but only by invoking another strange phenomenon, namely parthenogenesis, the development of eggs without fertilization by the male's spermatozoa. The parents were females of either *Poecilia (=Mollienisia) sphenops* or *Poecilia (=Mollienisia) latipinna*, the sailfin mollie. When males of either species would attempt to mate with females of the other species, the hybrid offspring were *Poecilia formosa*. These mollies are livebearers, so the sperm is deposited inside the female. But instead of fusing with the female's eggs, the sperm merely activates their development, resulting eventually in the birth of offspring that are all females.

Even normal sex determination gets to be pretty complicated in fishes. There are three sex determining chromosomes, symbolized as W, X, and Y. In some fish populations the combination XX produces a female and XY a male in a pattern that is familiar to us from mammalian genetics, including the case of human sex determination. In other populations, even of the same species, WY will combine to produce a female and YY will result in a male. The common element of the genetic make-up of males is the possession of the Y chromosome. The W and X chromosomes determine the female characteristics of the developing embryo, but whereas the Y chromosome is dominant over the X chromosome, W is dominant over Y, when they are combined. An interesting result of

Sexually dimorphic fish: the swordtail, *Xiphophorus helleri*; the upper fish is the female. Photo by G.J.M. Timmerman.

Sexually indistinct fish: brown discus, *Symphysodon aequifasciata*. Photo by Dudley Campbell.

these relationships occurred when an XX female platy *(Xiphophorus maculatus)* from the Rio Jamapa in Mexico was crossed with a YY male from the Belize river in Honduras. According to theory, only male offspring could result from such a mating and that is exactly what was found, one female producing 185 offspring, all males!

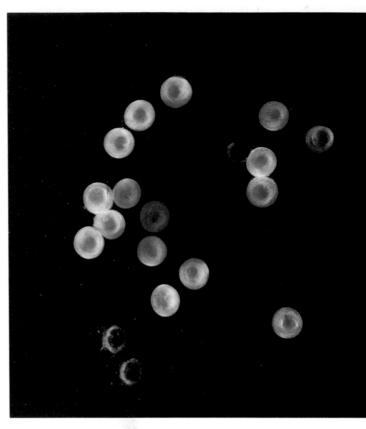

Adhesive type eggs of an albino catfish (*Corydoras aeneus*) attached to the side of a tank. Photo by Giancarlo Padovani.

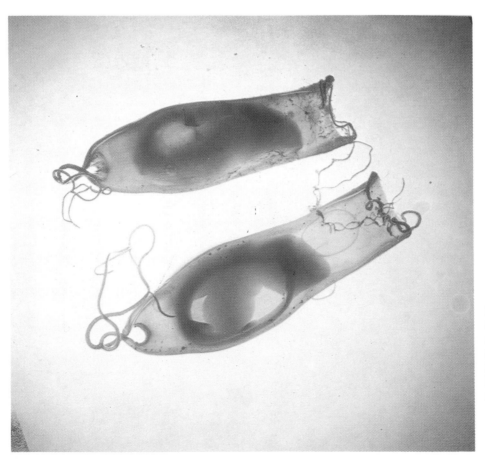

Egg capsules of a skate of the genus *Raja.* Each contains an egg which will hatch in four and one-half to fifteen months.

Fishes that care for their eggs, such as this African dwarf cichlid (*Pelvicachromis taeniatus*), lay fewer eggs than fishes that scatter their eggs freely. Photo by Hans Joachim Richter.

Chapter III

DEVELOPMENT AND MATURATION

The fish egg

All fishes start out life as an egg. How a single cell, and that is after all what an egg is, grows into an individual, a recognizable member of a species, yet not quite the same as any other, is one of the great mysteries of the universe. The interplay of genetic and environmental factors which brings about this development also helps the observer of fish behavior to interpret the functioning of the adult fish, as trace effects from earlier stages always survive to play a role in the behavior patterns of the mature individuals. We can see this effect of early environment in the way the salmon ascends the river in which it was hatched, rather than the one in which it was spawned, in order to breed. It can be observed as well in the modification of growth, the increased willingness to hybridize and the greater likelihood of breeding in captivity, that distinguish tank-raised aquarium fishes from their ancestors.

Development starts with fertilization of the egg. Most fish eggs are small and are shed into the surrounding water, while the male simultaneously discharges his sperm over the eggs or in close proximity. The spermatozoa are attracted chemically to the eggs, one of them penetrating the membrane surrounding the egg. Immediately on fertilization the membrane becomes impervious to the entrance of other sperm, thus insuring the union of only one spermatozoon, out of the millions available, with each egg.

In fishes that lay eggs, large numbers are the rule. A 54 pound ocean sunfish (*Mola mola*) is considered capable of producing 28,000,000 eggs in a spawning season; the cod (*Gadus*) lays as many as 9,000,000 eggs. These eggs float and receive no further care. The large number of eggs expelled assures that enough young survive to perpetuate the species, despite the huge attrition encountered under adverse conditions. Other fish have eggs that sink to the bottom, often adhering to plants or bottom gravel. The total number of eggs laid is much less than eggs of the floating type. Finally, fish that care for their eggs by building a nest, mouthbrooding or by keeping them in a brood pouch lay the least number of eggs.

Regardless of whether the egg is fertilized or not, it takes up water as soon as it is extruded from the female. The water uptake takes about an hour in the brook trout (*Salvelinus fontinalis*), somewhat shorter or longer in other species. At the same time the shell of the egg, which is soft when the egg is discharged into the water, starts to harden. This process takes 24 to 30 hours. Once the shell is hardened, the eggs are resistant to mechanical and chemical damage. A special exception is represented by the large, tough egg-cases secreted by skates and some sharks (Chondrichthyes).

Livebearers

Live young are born to many sharks and rays. Among bony fish, they are common among the toothcarps (Cyprinidontiformes), including such familiar aquarium favorites as the guppy, mollie, platy and swordtail (Poeciliidae). Other livebearers are found among the Goodeidae, Jenynsiidae, Anablepidae and the halfbeaks (Hemiramphidae). Live bearing also occurs in some surfperches (Embiotocidae), eelpouts (Zoarcidae), scorpionfishes and rockfishes (Scorpaenidae), as well as in brotulas (Brotulidae) and clinids (Clinidae) and one genus of sculpins, *Comephorus*. It probably exists in other fishes as well.

Long gestation periods and large young are typical of livebearing sharks. The spiny dogfish *(Squalus acanthius)*, for example, carries its one to fourteen young for two years, while the voracious white shark *(Carcharodon carcharias)*, which is common around Australia, gives birth to large young, weighing in at over 100 pounds.

These sharks nourish their developing young directly and are known as viviparous. Others give birth to live young, but their embryos develop within the oviduct and they are therefore considered ovoviviparous. An interesting behavior pattern is shown by the manta rays when they give birth to their live young. They leap out of the water as they eject their young, which tumble through the air before hitting the water surface.

Livebearing bony fish are generally called ovoviviparous, but their method of taking care of their embryos varies somewhat from that of the sharks and rays. The typical aquarium livebearers retain their eggs in the ovarian follicles. The ovarian follicle is the place where an ovum grows from a microscopic cell into a relatively large yolk-filled egg. In egg-layers the follicle ruptures during ovulation to release

The guppy, *Poecilia reticulata*, in the process of giving birth. The young usually emerge head first. Photo by F.M. Williams.

A male livebearer, the sphenops mollie, *Poecilia sphenops*. Photo by A. van den Nieuwenhuizen.

A large shark photographed off Sri-Lanka (Ceylon) by Rodney Jonklaas. Most of the sharks give birth to young alive.

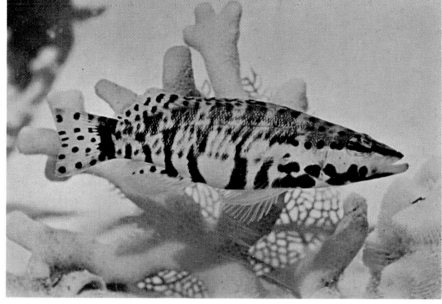

Sea basses (Serranidae) may be functional hermaphrodites. Note also the disruptive coloration (see p. 142) of this serranid, the harlequin bass, *Serranus tigrinus*. Photo by Dr. Herbert R. Axelrod.

A pair of sailfin mollies, *Poecilia latipinna*; the male is upper fish. Photo by Rudolf Zukal.

At birth young guppies straighten out from their curled-up position and rapidly swim away to hide, as their mother is quite likely to eat them. Photo by Chvojka Milan.

An unborn guppy can be seen peeking through the distended skin of its mother's gravid spot. Photo by Le Cuziat.

the eggs into the oviduct or directly into the body cavity in such exceptions as the female trout and salmon. In poeciliid livebearers, the fertilized ova are retained in the ovarian follicle and develop there up to the time they are expelled during birth, which is therefore technically speaking identical to ovulation. This mode of development is typical not only of the Poeciliidae, but also of the halfbeaks (Hemiramphidae) and four-eyed fishes (Anablepidae).

There are livebearers, on the other hand, that ovulate after the egg has been fertilized in the follicle, but retain their embryos within their ovaries. Special tissues provide nourishment directly into the gill cavity and mouth of the young (Jenynsiidae) or ribbon-like extensions grow out from the embryos into folds in the walls of the ovaries, as in the Goodeidae, Embioticidae and Brotulidae. Development of the embryo proceeds internally to various stages. Poeciliid livebearers are carried in a curled up position. At birth, which is usually head first, they straighten up and are capable of swimming almost immediately. They still carry a small yolk sac at this stage. Too large a yolk sac is a sign of premature birth and the young "hop" about on the floor of the aquarium instead of swimming away rapidly. Some livebearers, the surfperch *Cymatogaster* for example, sometimes carry their young internally all the way to sexual maturity.

How to hatch an egg

The fertilized ovum consists essentially of an outer tough protective membrane, the chorion, and an inner membrane, the vitelline membrane, the cytoplasm and nuclear material, and a supply of nourishing food for the developing embryo, the yolk. The development proceeds through various recognizable steps. The timing of these stages depends on a number of factors, temperature being the most influential. The most important steps are the division of the single cell into two, four, eight, sixteen and thirty-two cells, ultimately forming a layer of cells, the blastula, on top of the yolk. These cells can be shown to have differentiated already into regions which will form different organs and parts of the adult fish.

During the next stage, gastrulation, the blastula cells grow inward to form at first two and later three primitive layers from which all body tissues evolve. At the same time, other cells grow around the yolk to form the yolk sac. The body axis is formed and microscopic examination reveals the formation of the body segments, the somites. Subsequently the various organs of the body start to develop, the heart begins to beat and the fins can be observed to move. The development of the eyes is a very prominent feature. They can easily be seen in the developing embryo through the transparent egg membranes.

Hatching depends on the secretion by special cells of an enzyme that weakens or destroys the chorionic membrane. At the same time vigorous movement by the fins and gills facilitates the rupturing of the outer membranes. Development is by no means complete when the young are hatched. Most carry a yolk sac as food supply to tide them over the earliest period of post-hatching development. Frequently they attach themselves to plants or rocks or carry special flotation equipment. Shape and appearance may differ considerably from the adult form. These larvae may not even be recognized as belonging to the same species. The most famous case of mistaken identity concerns the larvae of the eel, which had been described as an entirely separate genus, *Leptocephalus*, before their true nature was recognized. To this day many species are probably incorrectly described from juvenile forms.

Early development

Rapid growth marks early development. An abundant food supply, after the yolk sac has been absorbed, is the most necessary

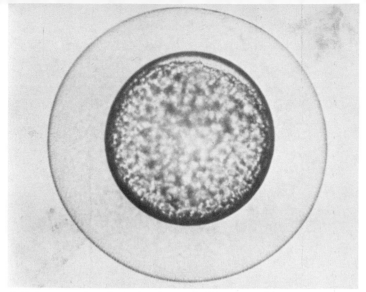

A fish egg, showing chorion, vitelline membrane and yolk sac.

The four-cell stage in a developing *Tilapia* egg. American Museum of Natural History photo.

A later stage of egg development in the eggs of the gaff-topsail catfish, *Bagre marinus*. The eyes are well developed, and a network of blood vessels surrounds the yolk sac. American Museum of Natural History photo.

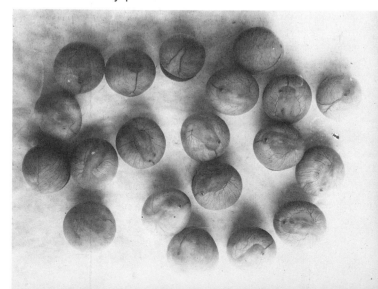

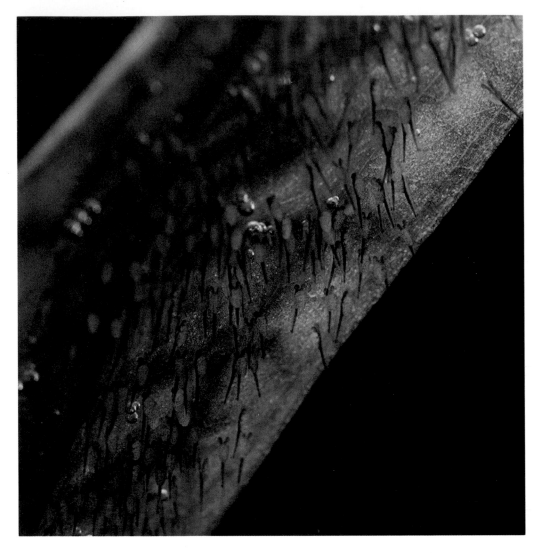

Larval stage young of *Trichopsis schalleri* soon after emerging from their nest attach themselves to a leaf, looking like tiny slivers and not at all like the adult.

A juvenile *Pseudotropheus zebra* on its way to assuming its adult form. Photo by Hans Joachim Richter.

Three stages in the development of the angelfish, *Pterophyllum scalare*. These are golden angelfish, a color variety. The group on top is about four weeks old, middle six weeks, bottom about two months. Photos by Peter Wong.

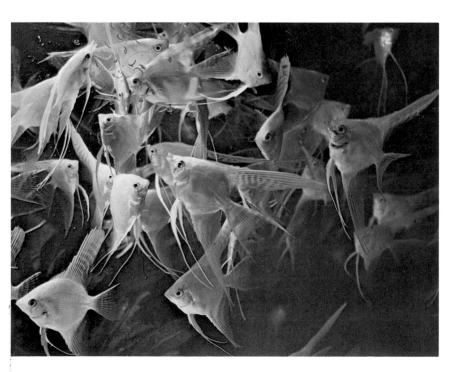

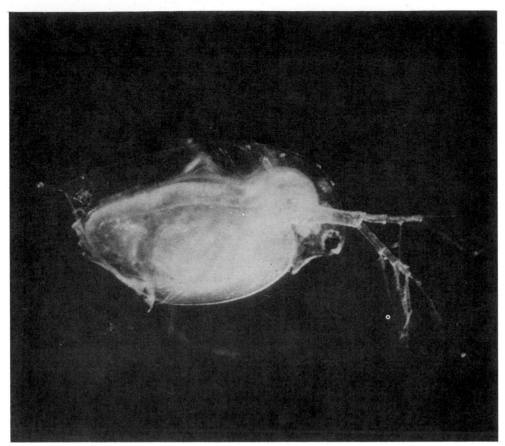

Enlarged picture of *Daphnia*, a favorite food for young fishes. Photo by Dr. Rolf Geisler.

ingredient. A suitable temperature and adequate water conditions also affect growth during this period, frequently called the larval or fry stage. Food must be of appropriate size and variety. The young, even of fishes that are strictly vegetarian as adults, require a high protein diet, made up primarily of very small single celled animals (infusoria), and the smallest of crustaceans (such as *Daphnia*) and insects. In this respect there is an interesting parallel to the young of seed-eating birds, which are also brought up on a diet of insects, worms and spiders, although as adults they subsist primarily on a vegetable diet.

It is normal for individuals to grow at widely differing rates. Before long, the fastest growing babies will begin to consider their smaller brothers and sisters as just another kind of live food. Because of this danger, fish culturists and professional aquarium breeders sort the young for size several times during the fry stage. Early size differences do not necessarily indicate the extent of final growth. When larger fry are removed, some of the smaller fishes grow very rapidly, catching up with and possibly even outstripping their former companions. It is thought that this differential growth may be caused by dominance relationships. Observations have shown that the larger fry act aggressively toward the smaller individuals and inhibit their feeding, even though abundant food is available. It is possible that the lack of growth can be attributed to the psychological stress associated with the inferior social status of the smaller fish.

Juveniles

Many fishes pass through a postlarval stage in which they differ from the adult both in physical appearance and behavior.

The physical features vary from distinctive coloration or transparency to entirely different shapes. Young angelfish *(Pterophyllum scalare)* and discus *(Symphysodon discus)*, for example, have a generalized fish shape at this stage and assume their flattened body and exaggerated fins only on maturation. Even more striking are the changes of the flatfishes (Pleuronectiformes), such as the flounders, that are bilaterally symmetrical as juveniles, before both eyes begin to move to one side of the body and other adaptations to a bottom dwelling life appear.

Most young fishes school, even in species which are solitary in adult life. It is thought that schooling provides an advantage in food seeking and a certain amount of protection from predation for the group as a whole.

Food supply, temperature and space are the three most important ingredients for achieving rapid growth. Growth is more satisfactory if the food supply exceeds the minimum necessary to maintain a healthy fish. As the fish mature, the relative amount of food required per unit of body weight decreases. In other words, young fish, like young children, need a relatively better diet than adults to maintain good condition and sustained growth.

Frequent feeding is considered more advantageous than larger meals at longer intervals. Appetite falls off above and below an optimum range of temperature. Below the optimum, fish are sluggish and do not feed readily. As temperature increases, their activity level increases; they eat more, but also need more food to sustain their more active metabolism. Above the optimum, appetite falls off, while the metabolism still demands a high food input, so growth rate slows down.

Growth has also been shown to depend on available space. Female guppies kept by themselves in identical conditions, except for container size, grew to a maximum size that depended on available space. When transferred to larger tanks, they resumed growth and reached a size typical for the larger container. Crowding many fish into a large tank has the same effect as giving each fish a smaller amount of space. There is, however, a beneficial effect in keeping a group of young together under uncrowded conditions. A certain amount of mutual stimulation increases feeding and promotes growth.

Maturity

Growth does not cease at maturity, judged to be the time when breeding activity becomes possible, although the growth rate slows down considerably at this time. Unlike the limitation imposed on the weight of mammals by the need to support their body on legs of limited load-bearing capacity, fish do not suffer any disadvantage from unlimited growth. Incidentally, whales, although mammals, also show this fishlike continued growth pattern.

The age at which sexual maturity is attained varies with the species and the conditions under which the fish was raised. Stunting a fish's growth results in maturation at a smaller size. In many cases aquarium raised fish mature at a much smaller size than wild-living specimens. For example, *Tilapia* species are raised as food fish in pond culture in many countries, where they grow to much larger size than tank raised individuals. Pond raised *Tilapia* also may mature much faster than those living in aquariums.

Senescence

In general, larger fish live longer than smaller fish. Also, as in humans, females have a longer life expectancy than males. Life spans vary. Annual breeders, such as *Cynolebias*, *Nothobranchius* or *Pterolebias* mature, breed and die within less than a year's time. Small livebearers, such as guppies, swordtails and mollies, typically reach an age of two to three years, as do *Betta*. Cichlids and barbs are longer lived, reaching an age of 10-15 years. Carps and goldfish may reach 30 years or more. The

A croaker (*Plagioscion squamosissimus*) demonstrating a very distinct lateral line (see p. 99). Croakers are very noisy fish (see p. 95). Photo by Dr. Herbert R. Axelrod.

Another croaker, the spotted drum, *Equetus punctatus*, shows a disruptive color pattern (see p. 142). The characteristic spots of the adult are not yet developed in this juvenile fish. Photo by Aaron Norman.

Toadfish (*Opsanus*) make a sound like a boat whistle (see p. 98). Photo by Aaron Norman.

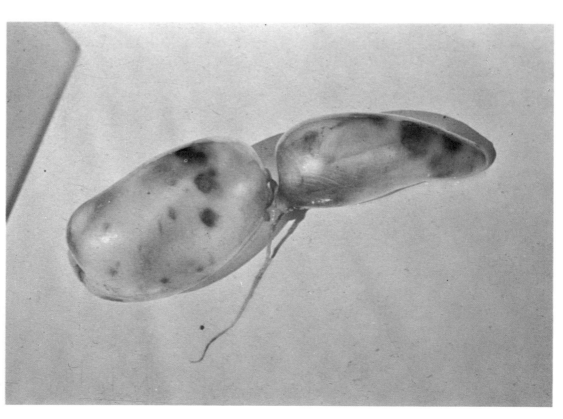

Swimbladder of the carp, *Cyprinus carpio*. The red spots are a sign of disease.

Males of *Poecilia nigro-fasciata* grow a hump on their back as they grow older. Photo by Chvojka Milan.

eel has been observed to live for 55 years. The European catfish *Silurus glanis*, long lived like all catfish, has a life span of 60 years or more, while a northern pike *(Esox lucius)* lived to at least 75 years in captivity.

Appearance and behavior may change with age. Some cichlids develop a pronounced hump on the neck with old age. Males of the Pacific salmon not only develop a humped back, but also elongated, hooked jaws. Colors may intensify, as they do in the salmon, or fade, as is the case in many cichlids. The fins take on a ragged appearance, as tears and injuries fail to heal as fast as they used to. Often senescent fish take on an emaciated, hollow-bellied appearance. Old fish become less active; with some exceptions they are less interested in breeding, and they find it more difficult to adjust to a new environment.

Fishes in the wild rarely live long enough to display the signs of old age. Predation and disease tend to eliminate them from the population before they reach this stage. It is true, though, that the highest mortality rates are found in the young. The age structure of a population depends on available food supply, disease resistance and predation. Comparative studies have shown that fishes raised in aquariums and fish ponds, where a steady food supply and tolerable living conditions are available, tend to outlive their wild brethren by a wide margin.

Chapter IV

VISION AND VISUAL BEHAVIOR

The sensory world

Animals live in a world that is directly dependent on their senses. Their knowledge of the environment is limited by the functioning and capacities of their sense organs, which provide them with information about their physical surroundings and the activities of other creatures around them. Friend or foe, prey or predator, must first be recognized by means of the senses, before appropriate action is possible.

Sensory input can be investigated by two mutually supplementary methods. Anatomical and physiological methods demonstrate the nature and function of the sense organs and, where accessible, can provide direct evidence that the stimulation of the sense organ was effectively translated into a train of nerve impulses carrying the coded information to the central nervous system.

Observational and behavioral methods, on the other hand, show that what happened in the environment was meaningful to the animal, as shown by the initiation or modification of its activity. The two methods do not necessarily agree. Electrophysiological recording may show nerve activity, but the strength of the signal may be too low to result in behavioral change or may be suppressed. It is also possible that observations show behavior for which no physiological receptor action has been demonstrated. For example, magnetic and electrical cues may be used in navigation, although no receptor is at present known for these forces in some of the fishes that seem to employ such means of orientation. Unraveling these apparent contradictions provides interesting opportunities for the scientist.

Fish optics

The sensitivity to visible light of the fish eye roughly corresponds to that of the human eye. Infrared and ultraviolet light, which do not effectively penetrate water, is not utilized. Responses to polarized light have recently been demonstrated in a number of species: halfbeaks, cichlids, salmonids and even goldfish.

Fish optics are complicated by the fact that water is often turbid, decreasing the distance at which objects can be seen. It is, therefore, not surprising to find that the fish eye has for a long time been considered to be very nearsighted. Recently this point of view has been challenged and it is best to leave the issue open at the moment.

The lens of the eye is almost spherical and focused by moving the whole lens toward the back of the eye. The human eye, for comparison, has a lens that is focused by changing its shape. Sharks appear to be an exception. Their eyes are farsighted and they accommodate by moving their lens forward. Some sharks also can contract their pupil, so that it forms a

Arowana fry with yolk sac. Fry resemble their parents. Photo by Dr. Herbert R. Axelrod.

An arowana, *Osteoglossum bicirrhosum*, showing eggs. Photo by Dr. K.H. Luling.

Discus (*Symphysodon*), here seen feeding from their parents' side. Fry do not look like their parents. Photo by Dr. Eduard Schmidt.

vertical slit, whereas teleosts have a fixed, round pupil, staring at their environment with the proverbial fish eye.

Special adaptations of the optical apparatus are found in a number of species. Best known is the four-eyes *Anableps anableps*, which swims at the surface with its eyes partially out of the water. Its eye has an egg-shaped lens with the greater curvature underwater and a lesser curvature above the water, somewhat like bifocal glasses. The pupil of the eye has a distinct horizontal dividing line, separating the two visual fields. Even more complex are the arrangements of some deep-sea fishes. One of them, *Bathylychnops*, has a large pair of upward-directed eyes and growing out of these, a pair of smaller eyes looking down and slightly to the rear. An internal flap divides the two chambers, so that a separate view is obtained by each. Talk about being "four-eyed!"

Shine a beam of light into a fish tank and you will find the eyes shining the light right back at you like little mirrors. The reflection is caused by a layer of cells, the tapetum lucidum, found primarily in freshwater species. It frequently is made up of reflective crystals of guanin, located in cells behind the light receptive layer of the eye. It might be added that fish don't particularly like to have a light shining directly into their eyes, especially after they have spent some time in the dark.

As mentioned before, most teleosts have a fixed pupil. Exposure to bright light starts two types of protective reaction to prevent glare and eye damage. Granules of the black pigment melanin move over the tapetum to block its mirror action. At the same time a photomechanical movement takes place inside the eye. The light receptors in the back of the eye consist of two types, rods and cones. The rods are the more light sensitive elements. When light hits the eye, melanin moves forward, at the same time as the rods move backward, burying themselves in the protective pigment layer. In dim light the reverse

Grunts (these are *Haemulon flavolineatum*) generate sounds by grinding their pharyngeal teeth, amplified by their swimbladder (see p. 95). Photo by C. Limbaugh.

Very prominent eyes mark the striped squirrelfish (*Adioryx diadema*). They are nocturnal feeders. Photo by Dr. Herbert R. Axelrod.

process takes place as the eye adapts to the darkness. Dark adaptation is a relatively slow process; light adaptation is much more rapid. In the Pacific salmon, for example, light adaptation is complete in 20-25 minutes; dark adaptation takes about an hour.

Rods absorb light by means of a photochemical reaction. The details of this process have been worked out in a series of brilliant researches. The chemical structure of the photosensitive substance, comparable to the sensitized layer on the films used in a camera, is now identified. Most marine fishes have been found to have a chemical system based on rhodopsin, also known as visual purple, the same system that is present in the human eye. Many freshwater fishes, on the other hand, utilize a system based on another substance, called porphyropsin. Fishes that migrate

from the ocean to fresh water, such as the salmon, change from a rhodopsin to a porphyropsin base prior to ascending their spawning runs.

Cone vision is not as yet understood as well as rod vision. Cones are necessary for seeing colors, while rods appear to be responsible only for vision in black and white, but many problems remain. Most sharks and rays probably have only rods and therefore presumably do not differentiate colors. Teleosts have both rods and cones, except for some deep-sea fishes, which lack cones. Color vision has been demonstrated in a number of species. Further analysis has shown that three different color receptors occur, with maximum sensitivity in the red, green and blue regions of the spectrum. Three receptor types are sufficient to represent all colors, as can be seen by the similar workings of color printing, color film and color television, which are all based on a mixture of three primaries.

What the fish eye sees

Fishes have good all around vision with a field of view that extends back to their tails, all around their sides and is capable of fused binocular seeing in front. Anyone who has observed aquarium fishes feeding or tending eggs has seen the coordinated movements of both eyes as they peer at a morsel of food or a batch of eggs. As a rule, fishes that swim around very actively show less coordinated eye movement than fishes that often stand motionless and tend to scan their environment with their eyes alone. It might be added that this behavior gives the fish a more alert appearance. Compare an ever active goldfish with a deliberately moving cichlid, such as an angelfish or an oscar. Some fishes, such as some catfishes, can move each eye independently of the other, presumably making it easier for them to keep an eye out for significant events in their environment, as their food is mainly found by tactile and chemical means.

The eyes can be rotated to a greater or lesser degree, depending on the species, to compensate for pitch, roll and yaw, thus providing a steady visual platform. Experiments have shown that horizontal and vertical lines are easier to discriminate for fishes than oblique targets. These differences may have something to do with maintaining a constant frame of reference for living in a three-dimensional world. Visual orientation must take into account the fish's own movement in relation to its environment, in order to judge current, relative drift and avoid obstacles. For this reason, visual cues are integrated with receptors in the lateral line and labyrinth.

Most fishes apparently see very well under water; but blinded fishes manage to avoid obstacles and find food without any apparent trouble. Some fishes have reduced or weak eyes, for example, the catfish *Ictalurus nebulosus*, and completely degenerate eyes occur in the blind cave fish *Astyanax mexicanus*, a blind African barb, and a number of deep-sea species. Some deep-sea fishes, however, have very much enlarged eyes, even though they live at depths where sunlight never penetrates. It is speculated that they are dependent on light given off by the special light producing structures found in many of their fellow deep-sea fishes.

Fishes can also see in air. The four-eyed fish *Anableps*, which has an optic system that simultaneously scans the environment above and below the water surface has already been mentioned. Mudskippers, such as *Periophthalmus*, a fish that is happy to spend many hours out of the water, have special folds into which they retract their eyes to keep them moist when outside the water. They can see well enough in air to hunt for their food in the tangle of mangrove roots above the mud flats of estuaries and tidal river mouths, where they like to live. The rockskippers (*Mnierpes*) climb about their rocky tidepools, well aware of their surroundings, thanks to their flattened corneal surfaces, which divide their eyes into anterior and posterior windows. Flat corneas are also found in the eyes of the blenny *Entomacrodus nigricans* and the flying fish *Cypselurus heterurus*.

Most fishes, of course, have to spend all their lives under water. When they attempt to look out into the air, they have to cope with the problem of light refraction at the water surface. This difference in light refraction is the cause of the bend that appears in the handle of a net that is dipped into a tank when trying to catch a fish. It limits the horizon of a fish looking out of the water to a visual field of only 97° of angle, instead of the normally expected 180° field. Beyond this window total reflection causes a mirror-like appearance of the surface. Ripples on the water surface cause additional fractionation of the view, making multiple images of any environmental objects.

Steatocranus casuarius, the lion-head cichlid. A young pair of breeders. In old age the bump on the head becomes exceedingly large in this species (opposite page, bottom).

The red devil, *Cichlasoma erythraeum*, develops a hump on the neck, as well as very prominent lips, when mature. Photo by Mervin F. Roberts.

A mature Jack Dempsey, showing the hump that develops at the nape at maturity. Photo by Stanislav Frank.

Young Jack Dempseys, *Cichlasoma octofasciatum*. Photo by Harald Schultz.

Steatocranus casuarius, adult male. Photo by Dr. Herbert R. Axelrod.

The brown bullhead, *Ictalurus nebulosus*, has poor eyesight but compensates by its acute sense of hearing, smell and taste. Photo by Gunter Senfft.

Despite these handicaps, fishes make use of features outside the water. The characin *Copeina arnoldi* deposits its spawn above the water surface and stations itself below its eggs to splash them with water in order to prevent them from drying out. The archer fish *Toxotes jaculator* shoots down insects that are within range by means of a well-aimed stream of water that knocks them down from their perch to be readily gobbled up by the successful hunter. Archer fish are not always successful, but are able to improve their aim through practice. Many fishes are thought to practice celestial navigation, making use of the sun or other celestial bodies to establish their position.

Extra-optic light reception

The eyes are not the only organ by which fishes respond to light. It has been known for some time that a brain structure, the pineal organ, is sensitive to light reaching it through the roof of the skull. Lampreys and hagfishes (Agnatha) actually have pigment cells and a lens-like structure above the pineal organ. Teleosts may have a pigment spot over the location of the pineal. The function of this light receptor is not well understood. It plays a role in the regulation of body function through release of light-dependent secretions. There is also some evidence that it may alter the responsiveness to light received by the eyes. It does not function as a third eye, in the sense that the fish cannot learn to associate light received by the pineal with other cues or form an image. But it does seem to be necessary for the smooth functioning of many of the processes that are dependent on light, such as daily activity cycles.

Chapter V

HEARING AND SOUND PRODUCTION

Underwater sound

Of all possible physical forces that could be used to provide information about the environment, sound is the most efficient for underwater purposes. Yet for many years the scientific world believed that fishes were deaf, and far from recognizing their capacity for sound production, the proverbial "silent sea" was the accepted majority opinion.

Sound is the result of physical vibrations of a medium. We are used to sound transmitted by air, a relatively thin medium that is inferior in transmission properties to water, a much denser medium, in which sound waves travel almost five times as fast as they do in air. It takes more energy to get sound waves started in water, but once set in motion, underwater sound travels long distances with very little loss and at high speed. Long distance transmission of sound waves is aided, in addition, by reflection from the water surface, the bottom, and from the boundaries of layers of water at different temperatures. On the other hand, there is also a lot of extraneous noise in any body of water, due to waves, friction of moving water, and the shifting of sand and other loose objects by currents and wind. For example, a calm sea has about the same acoustic pressure level, measured in decibels, as a normal conversation at one yard. A rough sea produces as many decibels as a small propeller driven airplane. Compare this noise to measured fish sounds. A chorus of marine catfish reached the acoustic pressure of a New York subway train at 30 yards and the boat whistle sound of the toadfish *(Opsanus tau)* equalled that of a loud automobile horn.

Fishes take advantage of these underwater vibrations in many ways. Low frequencies are detected by the lateral line. These may be considered low pitched sounds, as well as vibrations set up by obstacles, currents or approaching fish. The fact that the ear is not involved in receiving these signals has caused some argument that they should not be considered true sounds. But the finding that the acoustic nerve innervates both the inner ear and the lateral line, as well as the evolutionary history of the hearing apparatus, which shows that it is derived from the lateral line, argues for the interpretation of at least some of these low frequency vibrations as sounds.

Fish acoustics

Three structures that take part in the reception of acoustical stimuli by fishes are the inner ear, the swim bladder and the lateral line. The nature of underwater sound reception is further complicated by the presence of two types of effects of vibrating sources of acoustical energy, one due to the displacement of water particles, the other due to pressure waves. These are known as the "near-field" and the "far-field" respectively. They normally occur together and are difficult to separate.

The eyes of this four-eyed fish (*Anableps anableps*) protrude from the water as the fish surveys its environment. Photo by W.A. Tomey.

A mudskipper (*Periophthalmus barbarus*) has found a comfortable perch from which to watch his surroundings. Photo by Hilmar Hansen, Aquarium Berlin.

The inner ear of fishes is built along the same pattern as that of other vertebrates. It consists of three semicircular canals, serving the equilibrium sense and the otolith organs that are sensitive to vibrations. Instead of a cochlea, fishes have three sacs that are filled with a fluid called endolymph, each containing an earstone, the otolith. The otoliths differ for different fish species and are useful in classifying fishes. They also show annual growth rings and thus may be used to diagnose a fish's age. Fishes have no eardrum or middle ear.

In some fishes, notably the Cypriniformes (superorder Ostariophysi), such as the characins, knifefishes, minnows, loaches and catfishes, there is a chain of small bones, the Weberian apparatus, connecting the swim bladder to the inner ear. Members of this order appear to have the best hearing. These little bones remind one of the structure of the human middle ear with its chain of bones which convert air pressure vibrations into displacement of fluid in the human inner ear. Other orders of fishes have various extensions and connections of their swim bladder that reach the region of the inner ear and presumably have an auditory function. Although the swim bladder seems to be the best detector of sound pressure that fishes

Converging eye movements permit this flag cichlid, *Aequidens curviceps*, to examine the aquarium bottom for developing young by binocular vision. Photo by Hans Joachim Richter.

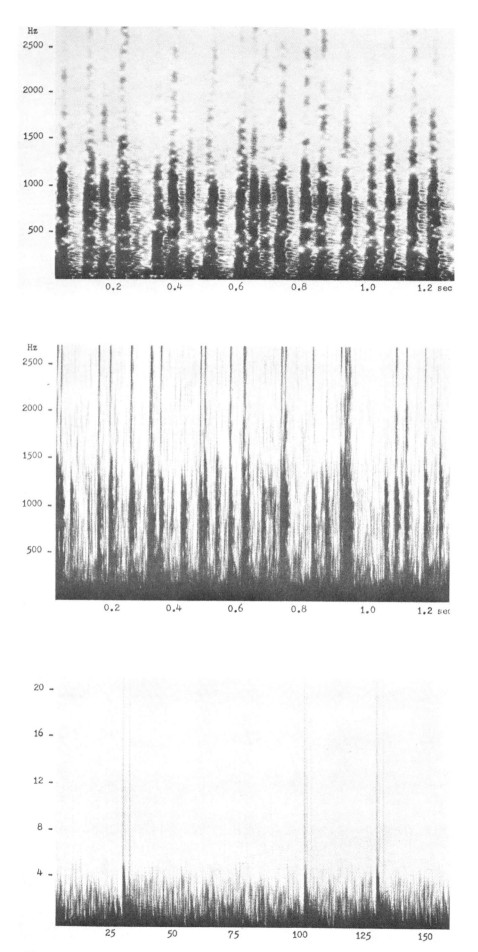

Sound spectogram of short pulse burst sounds of a group of 18 captive sea catfish (*Galeichthys felis*). Analysis band width 45 Hz.

Spectogram of the same sounds as top figure, but with a wider analysis band width of 300 Hz.

The same spectogram on an expanded time scale. Effective band width, 2400 Hz. These pulse burst may contain information that could tell the fish about its immediate environment and the presence of obstacles. (From William N. Tavolga, Acoustic orientation in the sea catfish, *Galeichthys felis. In* H.E. Adler (ed.) Orientation: Sensory Basis, *Annals N.Y. Acad. Sci.*, Vol. 188, pp. 80-97.)

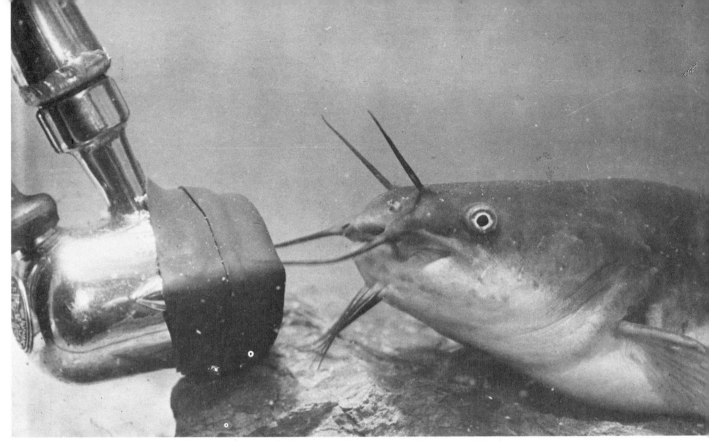

A brown bullhead, *Ictalurus nebulosus*, investigating microphone. Photo by Lilo Hess.

possess, there must be an alternate mechanism. Sharks lack a swim bladder, but hear nevertheless, thus presenting scientists with the opportunity for some more detective work.

It is now recognized that the swim bladder and inner ear comprise a system that allows the fish to hear the higher frequencies of their range and is sensitive to the pressure waves of the far-field. It is probably a non-directional detector system. Low frequencies are "heard" by means of the lateral line, a near-field receptor of displacement of water particles. The lateral line consists of a series of sensitive hair cells that are bent by changes in water motion. They exist as free receptors in the skin, but in many fishes they occur along a well defined canal, running along the trunk and branching at the head. The lateral line system is capable of resolving the direction of a sound source, but is limited in its effectiveness by the sharp dropping off of the near-field with distance. A rough analogy of the fish's hearing system would be the hi-fi loudspeaker's woofer and tweeter, the former reproducing low sounds, the latter the high frequencies.

What the fish ear hears

Fishes are sensitive primarily to lower frequency sounds. Their most efficient hearing range extends from about 200-600 Hz (cycles per second). This span is best visualized, if you consider that the middle C on the musical scale corresponds to 256 Hz and an octave represents a doubling of this frequency, so that C above middle C would be 512 Hz, for example. Human speech sounds have their basic components in the frequency range from 300-3000 Hz. Above 1000 Hz hearing sensitivity of fishes falls off rapidly. Compare this range to the human ear's top sensitivity in the range of 2000-4000 Hz and upper limit of 20,000 Hz, at least for young people's ears. Still higher frequencies, inaudible to the human ear, are heard easily by porpoises. The bottlenosed porpoise *(Tursiops truncatus)*, for example, has its best hearing range

The blind cave fish, *Astyanax mexicanus,* has lost its sense of sight but gets along very well without it. Photo by D. Terver.

The bubble-eye, a fancy goldfish variety. Photo by Hilmar Hansen, Aquarium Berlin.

The seaweed blenny, *Blennius marmoreus*, lives in shallow water areas with rocky bottom with algal growth. Some blennies occasionally crawl out of the water and hop on the rocky shore. Photo by Aaron Norman.

Flyingfishes (*Cypselurus poecilopterus* shown here) probably can see quite well in air. Photo by Dr. Shih-chieh Shen.

from 50,000-70,000 Hz and an upper limit above 135,000 Hz. Porpoises, by the way, are aquatic mammals, not fish.

Even at the frequencies where their hearing ability is best, fishes require a loudness that is considerably above the human threshold before a response can be obtained. An interesting observation that has occasionally been made, when testing for sound intensity thresholds, has been the splitting of the threshold into two levels, separated by about 20 decibels. The lower of these thresholds has been interpreted as due to the lateral line system, the higher as due to the auditory system.

Hearing sound is one thing, being able to distinguish between different sounds is something else. Fishes have a limited hearing range, but do well when tested on sound discrimination. The minnow *Phoxinus* was able to distinguish sounds about a quarter of a note apart. Goldfish do about as well. Fishes that do not have the Weberian apparatus of the Cypriniformes did more poorly in tests of sound discrimination.

Low frequency sounds, especially sounds in the range produced by the thrashing of a wounded fish, are attractive to predators, particularly to sharks. Sounds may also serve as a warning signal for other fish to stay away. This kind of function has been found, among others, in groupers, squirrelfish and toadfish. Still other sounds may serve as mating calls. Best known are the rattling sounds of the drumfish *Aplodinotus*.

Experiments showed that the European minnow, *Phoxinus phoxinus*, was able to distinguish tones about a quarter of a note apart. Photo by Gunter Senfft.

A sound-producing characin, *Glandulocauda inequalis*. The clicks of this fish can be heard when it comes to the water surface. Photo by Harald Schultz.

Male toadfishes *(Opsanus)* produce a loud, low "boat-whistle" to attract the female. Other fishes that have been heard to emit sounds during reproduction include some freshwater minnows, the characin *Glandulocauda inequalis*, and some cichlids. Much more information is needed on what use sounds are to fishes. Often it is known that fishes are capable of producing a sound, but virtually nothing is known about the meaning of this sound to other fishes.

Sound production

Roughly two types of fish sounds can be distinguished. High pitched sounds are described as squeaks, chirps, rasps or clicks. Low pitched sounds, on the other hand, are variously called croaks, thumps, bleats, rattles, yelps, grunts or buzzes. The distinctions depend on the means by which the sound is produced and on whether the sound is a single burst of energy or a continued pattern.

One common means of sound production is the rubbing together of hard surfaces. These so-called stridulatory sounds are often produced by the gnashing of teeth. That is the method used by the croaking gourami *(Trichopsis vittatus)* in connection with its courtship and territorial behavior. It is also the way sound is produced by grunts (Pomadasyidae) and squirrelfishes (Holocentridae). The swim bladder of these fishes often serves as a resonator, changing the sound quality. The triggerfishes (Balistidae) may also use their swim bladders to change the nature of their sounds, which in their case originates in the movement of two bones in the pectoral girdle.

The aptly named drums and croakers (Sciaenidae) vibrate the walls of their swim bladder by means of specialized muscles. Mature males produce a drumming sound. Their choruses were loud enough to interfere with acoustic mines laid in

The croaking gourami, *Trichopsis vittatus*, makes sounds by gnashing its pharyngeal teeth. Photo by Hans Joachim Richter.

Although lacking a swimbladder, sharks, such as this gray reef shark, *Carcharhinus amblyrhynchus*, are able to hear underwater sounds. Photo by Dr. Gerald Allen.

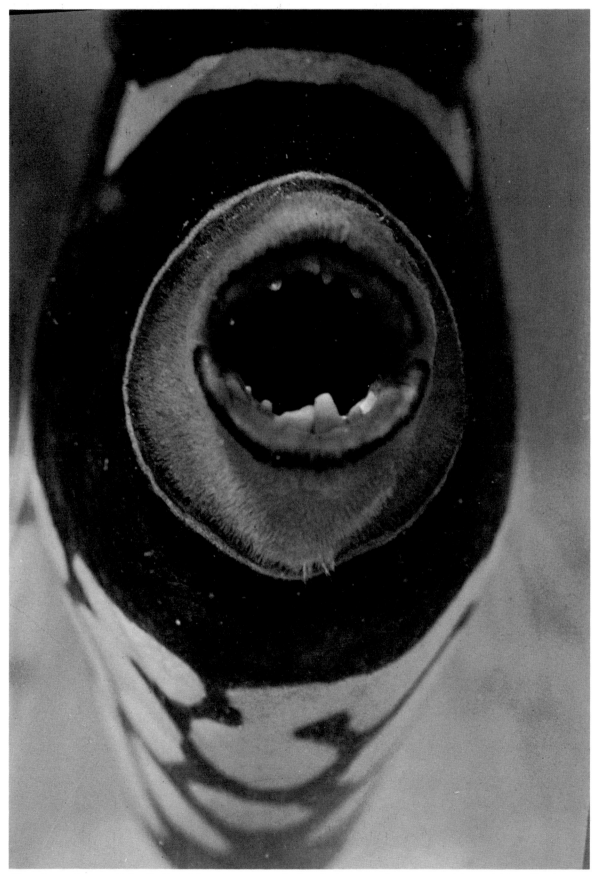

The clown triggerfish, *Balistoides niger*, seen in front view, produces sound by rubbing the bones of its pectoral girdle together. Photo by Dr. Herbert R. Axelrod.

A pair of blind cave fish, *Astyanax mexicanus*. This species is also known as *Anoptichthys jordani*. Photo by Gunter Senfft.

Tokyo harbor during World War II. Their activity is seasonal, peaking in June, and diurnal, starting about 5 p.m. in the afternoon, reaching its maximum at about 10 p.m. and dying down at 2:30 a.m. At its maximum, their chorus has been described as "being of the same order of magnitude as an airplane motor 15 feet away."

Many other species utilize a similar method to set their swim bladder into vibration. Among them are many of the catfishes, particularly the gafftopsail catfish *(Bagre marinus)* and the sea catfish *Galeichthys felis*. The sea catfish is capable of a considerable noise output. At night, their choruses have been compared to the "bubbling of a giant percolator." It is possible that some of their sound is employed for a form of echolocation. If this capability is confirmed by future research, it will be the first fish for which this mechanism, now only known for bats, porpoises and some birds, will have been demonstrated.

The swim bladder itself may have the appropriate musculature to serve as an organ of sound production. The toadfish *Opsanus tau* uses it to make a very loud noise that has been compared to a boatwhistle or a fog horn. Their blasts constitute a veritable chorus during their spawning season, late May to early June off Rhode Island, and to the end of October in Chesapeake Bay. The midshipman *(Porichthys notatus)* utilizes a similar mechanism to produce its grunts and buzzes.

Not too much is known, as was mentioned, of the function of many of the sounds that fishes make. Probably the best understood reasons are connected with courtship and spawning. For example, the male goby *Bathygobius soporator* will approach the playback of the sounds of another male. Defense of the nest, fighting displays and coordination of spawning synchronization between the sexes appear to be other functions. Among other observations of behavior that seemed to be correlated with fish sounds were territorial defense, schooling, escape from danger and migration.

Chapter VI

LATERAL LINE AND LABYRINTH

Water pressure and currents

The lateral line and associated sense organs form a unique system, found only in fishes and the aquatic stages of amphibians, such as tadpoles, for example. It plays a unique role in acoustic orientation, as we have seen. In evolutionary history it is of great importance as the most likely origin of the inner ear and the development of hearing in higher vertebrates.

In addition to its sensitivity to near-field displacement, the lateral line system provides information regarding laminar flow and surface eddies. The detecting elements are hair cells which are displaced or bent by mechanical forces. These sense organs which are located in the lateral line canal proper also appear as free groupings on the head and on lines along the body, in pits distributed over head and body, and in partially open or closed canals. The hair-cell receptors themselves are enclosed in very thin and flexible protective gelatinous capsules.

At present, there is no complete agreement on the capabilities of the lateral line system in making use of water currents. Fishes have been found to be sensitive to currents caused by the motions of other animals at short distances, presumably due to lateral line detectors. It is not clear whether the lateral line also plays a role in maintaining individual positions in a school of fish. Obstacle avoidance may be mediated by the lateral line. When a fish approaches an object, the current pattern is disrupted, changing the pressure distribution in such a way that lateral line receptors may be stimulated. Blinded fishes, as well as fishes with non-functional eyes, such as the blind cave characin *Astyanax mexicanus* , also known as *Anoptichthys jordani* , navigate by means of the lateral line system, utilizing particularly the organs located in the head region.

Surface feeders become aware of a fly struggling on the water surface and home in on their prey by sensing the surface waves by means of lateral line organs in the head region. Different parts of the lateral line receptor system are tuned in specific directions, forming a series of overlapping perceptual fields. Experiments with blinded specimens of the striped panchax *(Aplocheilus lineatus)* and the black-striped killifish *(Fundulus notatus)* showed that they responded immediately when the propagated surface wave reached their position, but never appeared to react to the much faster moving sound wave. The accuracy of localization was best at short distances, reaching a maximun of 86.5 per cent strikes correctly on target to a single disturbance. Continuous waves, as might be produced by a real struggling insect, were located with even better precision.

One more function of the versatile lateral line system should be mentioned here, although it will be examined in more detail later. Three groups of weakly electric

A school of blue-striped snappers, *Lutjanus kasmira*. Photo by Pierre Laboute.

A mormyrid (*Mormyrus* sp.) photographed in a tank by Hilmar Hansen, Aquarium Berlin.

A newly caught bottlenose (*Mormyrus longirostris*) from Lake Malawi. Photo by Dr. Herbert R. Axelrod.

An upside-down catfish, *Synodontis nigriventris*.
Photo by G.J.M. Timmerman.

fishes (Gymnotoidei, Mormyridae and Gymnarchidae) have modified lateral line organs that detect the deformation of an electric field by objects in their vicinity. This electrolocating mechanism is an active sensory system, comparable to the sonar of bats, birds, cetaceans and possibly fishes. Passive electrosensory functions have also been found in catfishes, sharks and rays. Lateral line organs in these fishes are sensitive to electrical fields, although these fishes do not themselves appear to emit electrical impulses.

How to keep one's equilibrium

Fishes live in a three-dimensional world, where absence of light and lack of a fixed solid ground often pose a formidable

Striped panchax, *Aplocheilus lineatus*. Photo by Gerhard Marcuse.

problem in orientation. It is the function of the labyrinth to cope with this problem. The labyrinth of the inner ear consists of the semicircular canals and three pouch-like sacs containing the earstones or otoliths. These otoliths organs are known as the utriculus, sacculus and lagena. They are sensitive to gravity, as well as to vibrations. The· utriculus seems to be the primary element in the system, as far as response to gravity is concerned. At least, when sacculus and lagena are eliminated, responses to gravity remain. The three semicircular canals are filled with fluid. Their task is to sense acceleration in three cardinal directions.

Body balance is maintained by a system that involves not only the labyrinth, but the cyes as well, when light is available. Illumination falling on a fish from above causes the so-called dorsal light reaction, as the fish adjusts its posture to turn its back to the light source. After eliminating the utriculus, this reaction can be seen very clearly, by shining a light on a fish from its side or even the bottom. The fish will react by swimming on its side or upside down. Even in some intact fishes, the dorsal light reaction is easily seen, when a strong light is used to illuminate their tank from the side or below. Angelfish (*Pterophyllum*) are excellent subjects for this experiment, which any aquarist can easily carry out.

Entrance to La Cueva Chica, habitat of the blind cave fish, near the village of Pujal in San Luis Potosi, Mexico. New York Zoological Society photo.

Taste plays an important role in a fish's life: here a Hawaiian surgeonfish (*Acanthurus dussumieri*) nibbles on algae. Photo by Walter Deas.

Goatfish (*Mulloidichthys samoensis*) exploring the bottom. Photo by Allan Power.

Copperband butterflyfish, *Chelmon rostratus*, reaching inside a mussel. Photo by Dr. Anthony T.F. Teh.

Chapter VII

THE CHEMICAL SENSES: TASTE AND SMELL

Taste

Anyone who has watched a fish mouthing a piece of food, spitting it out again, taking it back into the mouth and finally either rejecting or accepting it, has no doubt about the important role that taste plays in a fish's life. There has been some argument whether taste and smell are two different functions, as fishes are constantly bathed in the chemical substances that may stimulate both types of receptors. Taste buds are located not only in the mouth, but also in the gill cavity, on the gill arches, on barbels and fins and, in some fishes, all over the body, to make things even more complicated. Experiments have clearly shown, however, that two separate senses are involved, as eliminating the olfactory lobes of the brain still permitted the fishes to discriminate tasty substances.

Fishes are very sensitive to the taste of food substances. The carp, for example, has very well developed taste organs on the roof of the mouth and lips, which enables it to sort through a mouthful of bottom sediment, retain the edible material and reject the rest. Fishes appear to have a sweet tooth. Minnows had a sensitivity to sugar 512 times better than the human taste threshold in one experiment. Catfish barbels can quickly identify food substances with which they come in contact.

Exposure to low concentrations of detergents seriously impaired their sense of taste, with recovery not fully complete after six weeks in detergent-free water.

Smell

The sense of smell in fishes varies over a wide range, depending on the development of their olfactory organs. Sharks and rays have highly sensitive pits on the bottom side of the snout. Water constantly passes through the organs when the fish breathes, as there is an opening connecting the intake and outlet, with the current in some cases leading into the mouth. Lungfishes also have a canal leading into the mouth from the external opening, which is on the upper surface of the snout in their case. Teleost fishes have their nasal opening also on the dorsal side of the head, but have no connection to the inside. In some cases, such as the eel, there is a long tube; in others, such as the minnows, there is an erectile skin flap, deflecting a stream of water into the nasal pit through an inlet opening and out of the pit through an exit opening. Other fishes, for example the stickleback *(Gasterosteus)* have only one opening through which the water is alternately taken in and expelled. Finally, there are some, highly visually guided fishes, such as some of the puffers (Tetraodontidae) that have no nasal pit at all.

The polka-dot African catfish, *Synodontis angelicus*, has very sensitive taste buds. For some unknown reason this species is attracted to rusty iron. Photo by G.J.M. Timmerman.

The barbels of the clown loach, *Botia macracantha*, indicate a well-developed sense of taste. Photo by Klaus Paysan.

At the bottom of the pit are receptor cells, arranged in a complicated series of folds. As might be expected, the complexity of the structure correlates roughly with the degree of olfactory sensitivity. Fishes that hunt by sight, such as the pikes *(Esox)*, have fewer cells than fishes that have a very acute sense of smell to guide them to food and in finding their way, such as the eel *(Anguilla)*. There is, at this time, no generally accepted explanation of the mechanism of smell reception.

Smell plays a major role in the life of fishes. Food is sought and found by smell in many instances. Catfish, for example, are capable of true olfactory searching, following a smell to its source, ultimately seizing it when their barbels make contact, as their sense of taste comes into play. Other fishes tend to swim against an odorous current, without necessarily following the gradient to its source. The odor of food merely triggers their swimming activity, which will normally lead them to the food source, as it will be directed upstream. The smell of food causes searching behavior and induces a feeding mood. Goldfish stimulated elec-

The northern pike, *Esox lucius*, hunts mainly by sight. It lacks a very sensitive sense of smell. Photo by Dr. D. Terver, Nancy Aquarium.

Sharks and rays such as this short-nose mud skate, *Rhina ancylostoma*, have their olfactory organs on the bottom side of the snout. Photo by Dr. Shih-chieh Shen.

Closeup showing the flapped nasal pit of a grouper (*Cephalopholis*). Photo by Dr. Herbert R. Axelrod.

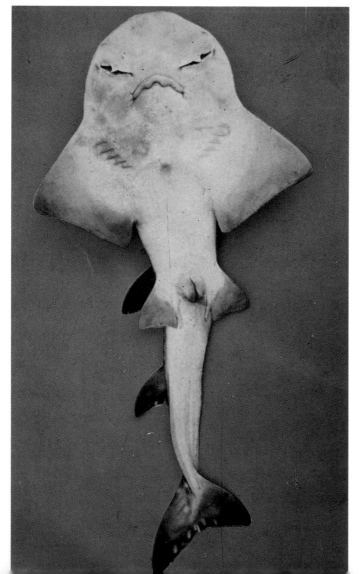

The three-spined stickleback, *Gasterosteus aculeatus,* has only a pair of nasal pits. Photo by Klaus Paysan.

Moray eels (*Gymnothorax* species shown here) possess the tube-like olfactory organ found in many eels. Photo by Dr. Gerald Allen.

A congregation of herbivorous African cichlids grazing on the luxuriant algal growth below 12 feet of water in Lake Malawi. Photo by Dr. Herbert R. Axelrod.

trically in the olfactory area of their brain engaged in feeding activity indistinguishable from normal behavior.

At least some fishes find their mates by olfactory means. The common bullhead *Ictalurus nebulosus* and the goby *Bathygobius soporator* engaged in courtship behavior in response to water that had contained a female in breeding condition. Chinook salmon *(Oncorhynchus tshawytcha)* showed electrical activity in the olfactory areas of their brain when stimulated by water that had contained other individuals of the same species. Minnows could distinguish the body odors of 15 different species of fish. They could also dis-

tinguish the odors of two species of frogs, as well as two species of salamanders.

Odors can be repellent as well as attractive. Salmon and trout were repelled by water in which human hands had been rinsed. Minnows exhibit an alarm reaction to some odorous chemical released by the injured skin of one of their own species. This alarming material goes by the terror inducing name of *Schreckstoff* (fright substance). The phenomenon seems to be confined to fishes of the order Cypriniformes. Fear reactions to the odor of intact predator species have also been demonstrated.

Chapter VIII

FEEDING AND FOOD SEEKING

The food chain

Fishes, like all other forms of life, form part of a chain of the eaters and the eaten. At the beginning of the chain are the green plants, which form the food for the herbivores. These in turn are the food for the carnivores. To complete the chain, the waste products of fishes and their dead bodies are decomposed and form the raw material needed by the plants for proper growth. The food chain may be envisaged as a pyramid, with the large mass of plant life at the bottom and a small number of predators at the top. Obviously the number of predators can never exceed the number of the prey and the largest of the predators, forming the narrow pinnacle of the pyramid, base their total food intake on a wide variety of smaller creatures. This relationship plays an important part in the accumulation of toxic pollutants, for example organic mercury, which has been found in the meat of large predatory fishes, such as the swordfish.

Feeding patterns

Feeding patterns vary with the nature of the diet. Fry eat more or less continuously, as long as suitably sized organisms are available. Herbivores and omnivores eat at frequent intervals, carnivores, when opportunity presents itself, which may involve long periods between large meals. Voluntary starvation occurs at times, as when salmon ascend their home stream or when a mouthbrooding fish is incubating a batch of eggs.

A detailed breakdown of feeding behavior of the three-spined stickleback (*Gasterosteus aculeatus*) shows a number of typical phases. The food object, such as a small worm, is first visually fixed, then the body is oriented toward the prey, the fish approaches, picks up the food and either eats or rejects the worm. As long as food is available, this pattern is repeated ten to twenty times, followed by a pause. As the fish becomes satiated, the pauses lengthen and bouts of eating become interspersed with periods of other activity. Eventually feeding stops, its end probably signalled by the distension of the stomach.

When made more hungry by food deprivation, the feeding becomes more rapid, but the total length of a bout remains about the same, the speed-up being determined largely by the decrease in fixation time and mouthing of food. A somewhat parallel behavior pattern marks the course of satiation. The slowing down of food intake is due to increase in fixation time and mouthing of food; the total length of the feeding bout remains steady.

The precise nature of the feeding movements is determined by the structural adaptations of the species and the nature of the food. Readiness to feed depends on the nature of the food, its palatability, abundance and ease of access. Past history plays an important role. Many fishes can

Angelfish, cardinal tetras and a kissing gourami attracted by a clump of freeze-dried *Tubifex*. Photo by Dr. Herbert R. Axelrod.

Surgeonfishes (*Acanthurus*) feeding. Photo by Dr. Gerald Allen.

Damselfishes (Pomacentridae) feeding in coral reef. Photo by Dr. Gerald Allen.

A surface feeder, the silver hatchetfish, *Thoracocharax stellatus*. Photo by Dr. Herbert R. Axelrod.

be weaned from their natural food to substitutes in captivity, although some predators depend on the movement of living prey to initiate their feeding pattern and thus cannot be fed anything but living food without extensive training.

Although the feeding action, as presently analyzed, is frequently considered a fixed pattern, a finer detailed and variable structure is revealed by a more comprehensive series of observations. For example, when *Badis badis* feeds on *Tubifex* worms, the movement by which it extracts the worms from the gravel at the bottom of a tank has been considered to be completely stereotyped. More detailed study showed that the precise form of the movement varied, depending on the strength of the worm's attachment to the gravel. A loosely anchored worm is pulled out by the momentum of the forward movement of the feeding fish, but a securely fastened worm is levered out by the fish turning on its side and using its body as a lever. As any experienced aquarist could have predicted, there is nothing fixed about an action pattern, except for the basic purposive movement. Each act is modified to suit the circumstances.

Symbiosis

Feeding is usually associated with competition for food, but certain special relationships have evolved that result in mutually beneficial association between two organisms. One such relationship exists between certain small fishes serving as cleaners of larger fishes, feeding on their ectoparasites and dead tissue. This behavior is probably not a true symbiosis and will be taken up in detail under the heading of social behavior. A truly mutual

Anemonefish (*Amphiprion ocellaris*) approaching anemone. Photo by Klaus Paysan.

bond, of benefit to both parties, exists between certain damselfish *(Amphiprion)* and sea anemones, and between the large jellyfish known as the Portuguese man-of-war *(Physalia)* and the man-of-war fish *(Nomeus gronovi)*.

The sea anemone is a beautiful, flower-like animal, a member of the coelenterate phylum. Its tentacles are loaded with highly poisonous darts, the nematocysts, that pierce the flesh of any fish that they touch—except their friend, the damselfish! These fish live unscathed within the ring of tentacles, well protected from other predators. They dart forth for food, which they bring back to "their" anemone, possibly just to secure it against other fishes, but with the effect that the anemone shares in their food supply. These fishes are unable to survive in the wild long without the shelter of their anemone. The anemone can survive without the damselfish.

Observation of this relationship in captivity has solved the puzzling fact that the fish appear to be immune to the poisonous darts of their hosts. The relationship, it turns out, is based on an individual bond, established between fish and host by an elaborate acclimatization process. An anemone that has been isolated from other fish and a fish that has been separated from anemones for some time are put into an observation tank. Soon after being immersed, the anemone attaches itself to a suitable substrate and opens its tentacles. At first the fish stays away, then it gradually makes its acquaintance, brushing against the tentacles occasionally and jumping away instantly.

Obviously the fish gets stung, but it returns again and again to contact the fierce tentacles of the anemone. Gradually the number of stings decreases, as the anemone becomes acclimatized to the fish and after a period of time the fish rests contentedly within the embrace of his host. With the species of anemone normally associated with *Amphiprion xanthurus*, the

Clown anemonefish without their natural shelter would not survive long in the wild. Photo by Robert L. Straughan.

damselfish that was tested, the acclimatization took about 10 minutes. But even with anemones that normally never serve as host, acclimatization is possible in some cases, only it takes longer.

The mechanism of acclimatization has been worked out in another study. Apparently anemones produce substances that inhibit their nematocysts from discharging into their own tentacles, should they touch accidentally. Using radioactive tracer chemicals that were adsorbed by the mucus covering their tentacles, it could be demonstrated that these labeled chemicals were transferred to the body of the damselfish during the acclimatization process. By coating themselves with this protective layer of mucus, the damselfish make use of the anemone's own protective mechanism. As a further test, it could be shown that wiping the mucus off the fish' body caused it to lose its immunity. And the fish knew it too. It would not return to the anemone

A giant anemone, *Stoichactis giganteus*, in company of clown-fishes and damsel-fishes. Photo by Dr. Gerald Allen.

An anemonefish (*Amphiprion clarkii*), peering out of a forest of tentacles. Photo by Dr. Herbert R. Axelrod.

Cardinalfishes (Apogonidae) frequently seek shelter among the spines of the black sea urchin or other suitable invertebrates. Photo by Pierre Laboute.

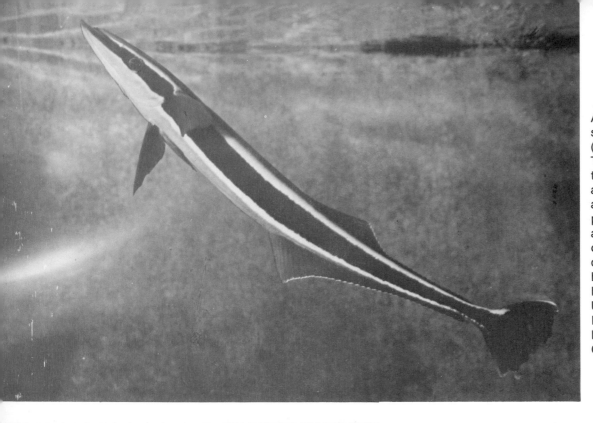

A remora or sharksucker (*Echeneis naucrates*). These fishes attach themselves to sharks and large fish, as well as to turtles, porpoises, whales and ships by means of a powerful suction disk on top of their heads (bottom left) to hitch a free ride. Upper photo by Miloslav Kocar, bottom photo by Gerhard Marcuse.

until it had gone through another acclimatization ritual.

Damselfishes are also observed occasionally to nibble on the anemone's tentacles. It may be that eating some of the nematocysts may produce a sort of immunity to the poison to protect the fishes from the few stings they receive during acclimatization. The man-of-war fish (*Nomeus*) similarly can also be observed tasting some of its protector's tentacles at times. The deadly sting of the Portuguese man-of-war is known to be capable of killing unacclimatized man-of-war fish that are subject to a massive dose of the jellyfish's poison. Under normal circumstances the fish is protected by its host's tentacles and fed by bits of food that are discarded by the jellyfish. *Nomeus* in turn may serve as a lure to attract unwary victims into the tentacles of the Portuguese man-of-war, thus providing the mutual benefit that is the hallmark of symbiosis.

The symbiotic relationship is not as clearcut in another example, that of the pearlfish *Carapus bermudensis* and the sea cucumber, a relative of the starfish and thus an echinoderm. Pearlfishes enter the cloaca

A sea cucumber (*Holothuria*) and a pearlfish (*Carapus bermudensis*) (bottom right) often found sheltering inside sea cucumbers. Although sea cucumbers secrete a noxious substance, pearlfishes are normally immune. Upper photo by Gerhard Marcuse, bottom photo by Dr. Walter Starck II.

of large sea cucumbers, such as the bêche-de-mer. They back into the opening tail first and use the echinoderm as shelter. The benefits accruing to the echinoderm are not known, so it is questionable whether a true symbiosis exists. Other species of pearlfishes hide in the shells of living oysters, hence the name. They occasionally become completely pearlized by their host.

Parasitism

Very few fishes are parasitic, in the sense that they depend on their host for their food supply. Best known are the two families of the class Agnatha, the jawless fishes. The lamprey *Petromyzon marinus* is an active, voracious vampire of the sea. They catch up with their victim, attach their sucker mouth, and rasp through the skin with their tongue. Their saliva contains an anticoagulant. They feast on the blood of their host and frequently weaken him to the extent that he eventually dies. An invasion of the American Great Lakes caused tremendous damage to the local fisheries industry. Lampreys are long-distance migrators. They are born in small freshwater streams, migrate to the ocean

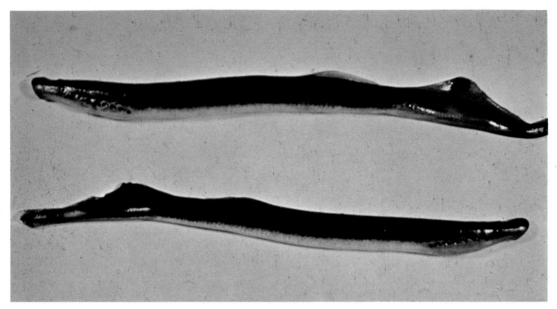

Lampreys are vampires of the fish world. Shown is *Lampetra fluviatilis.* Photo by Dr. H. Reichenbach-Klinke.

Like the man-of-war fish, this small fish, *Psenes pellucidus,* associates with a jellyfish, *Dactylometra pacifica.* Photo by Dr. Shih-chieh Shen.

(Top) Man-of-war fish, *Nomeus gronovi*, and (bottom) stranded Portuguese man-of-war, *Physalia physalia*, its shelter. Top photo by Dr. John E. Randall, bottom photo by Keith Gillett.

Goldfish being parasitized by candirú, *Vandellia cirrhosa*. Photo by Richard M. Segedi, Cleveland Aquarium.

where they mature, to return after a number of years to freshwater to spawn. Their journey up river is aided by their ability to use their sucker mouth to attach themselves to objects, enabling the lampreys to climb rapids and ascend waterfalls. Control of the lamprey pest in the Great Lakes depends on their breeding habits. Since these fishes are landlocked, they substitute the lake for the ocean to which they would normally return. By denying them entry to the small tributaries in which they spawn, their breeding cycle is interrupted and their population is now declining.

The second family, the hagfishes (Myxinidae) are scavengers as well as parasites. They enter dead or dying fishes by boring a hole in the skin of their victim and eat the insides until only a sack of skin is left. They lack eyes and apparently locate their prey by smell. They live in the ocean and do not enter fresh water.

Another parasitic fish can be quite dangerous to man, unlike the lampreys and the hagfishes, which have not been known to attack humans. The candirú (*Vandellia cirrhosa*) is a small eel-like South American catfish, that is more feared by the natives than the supposedly blood-thirsty piranha. It is usually parasitic on larger fish, entering their gill cavity and sucking their blood. But it can enter any other opening, such as the penis or vagina of humans venturing into infested waters. Candirús may become lodged in their victims' urethra or bladder, held fast by erectile spines on their gill covers. Once fixed in position, they cannot be dislodged, except by an operation, even though they may have suffocated, causing their host almost unbearable pain and suffering. A relative, the catfish *Stegophilus insidiosus*, lives in the gill cavities of large armored catfishes, where it feeds on the blood from wounds that their small rasping teeth produce in the gills of their host.

Still another kind of parasitism is based on sex. The male deep-sea anglerfish (*Photocorynus spiniceps*) spends almost his entire adult life as a parasite of its female. At some time after hatching the free-swimming larval male finds a female and attaches himself to her body. His mouth fits over a papilla, grown by the female, through which he absorbs nourishment. His own digestive system degenerates. The much smaller male spends the rest of his life in the company of his mate, having only one remaining function, to fertilize her eggs.

Chapter IX

FIGHTING AND DEFENSES

Individual space and territoriality

Any aquarist, experienced or novice, who looks at his fish tank with open eyes, can observe that his finny friends spend much of their time nipping and chasing each other, although little or no lasting damage results from this aggressive activity. The result of this interaction is a spacing out and distribution of fishes in specific parts or levels of their habitat. The key concepts related to these behavior patterns are territoriality, individual space and dominance hierarchies. Territoriality refers to a specific place which a fish will defend as his own place in the world. Many fishes, but by no means all, take up a territory at some time of their life, usually in connection with courtship and breeding, or a hiding place, or perhaps to secure and hoard some food.

Individual space refers to the space that a fish will attempt to keep clear around itself. It differs from territoriality in that it is not attached to any particular location. Defense of a territory is typified by a cichlid chasing all comers away from a spawning site, while individual space is exemplified by a school of characins, each individual holding his own position in the group.

Dominance relationships develop within any group; they determine who is boss and who follows next in line, until a very definite pecking order has been established. Depending on many factors, such as the species, number of individuals in the group, age and sex composition, and availability of space, these orders may be linear, triangular or of more complex form. Sometimes a super-bully will reign in a tank, holding all other members of his community in check to the point where they never get a chance to establish a hierarchy among themselves.

The newcomer or stranger is particularly vulnerable to attack. Adding any fish to an established tank carries the risk that the resident population will gang up on the new arrival and cause some damage to fins and scales. Often a pugnacious tyrant in a fish tank can be restrained by transferring him into another aquarium where he will be the stranger and consequently at the bottom of the ladder.

Much of the fighting that occurs between members of a species is of a highly ritualized pattern. Frontal and lateral displays alternate with fin slapping, tail beating and grasping of jaws. Colors are intensified and fins are spread. Each fish tries to appear as large and conspicuous as possible. When one of the combatants is ready to give up the fight, the colors fade, fins are clamped and the fish tries to flee his opponent's vicinity. In most cases no serious damage results, especially if the loser can put enough distance between himself and his antagonist to get out of the winner's territory.

Best known of aggressive fishes is of course the Siamese fighting fish, *Betta splendens*. A domesticated descendant of a

Tattooed eels, (*Muraena grisea*), sharing a hiding place. Photo by Hilmar Hansen, Aquarium Berlin.

This false cleaner (*Aspidontus taeniatus*) has taken up a territory inside a bottle. Photo by Allan Power.

A clingfish (*Lepadichthys lineatus*) on one of the arms of a feather star (Crinoidea). Photo by Dr. Victor Springer, U.S. National Museum of Natural History.

African dwarf cichlid (*Pelvicachromis taeniatus*) guarding its young. Photo by Hans Joachim Richter.

Betta splendens in combat. Photo by G.J.M. Timmerman.

Male Malawi cichlid (*Pseudotropheus auratus*) in defense of his territory against another male. Photo by Dr. D. Terver.

plain-looking, short-finned ancestor, a male *Betta* makes a splendid appearance in full fighting trim, with its blues, greens and reds at their most intense, all fins expanded and gill covers raised to their greatest extent. The female is less glamorous in appearance, as it often happens in the animal world, but still pretty pugnacious and an aggressive fighter.

Within seconds of being placed together, two males will begin their display. A mirror will do, when only one fish is available. (It is never a good idea to keep two males within sight of one another, as they will be displaying almost constantly.)

Their colors darken and intensify as each alternately circles the other or turns to face the other with his gill covers spread so that the normally hidden branchiostegal membrane becomes visible. The pectoral fins beat at a higher frequency than prior to the encounter. The pelvic fins are flicked back and forth. In particular, when two males display broadside, the pelvic fin on the side away from the adversary flicks forward and backward. The tail beats rapidly or flashes open and closed. The fish dart at each other with open mouth, threatening to bite, usually directing their onslaught at the other's tail. Although most attempts miss, tears in the tail fin are commonly found, when one of the combatants could not move it out of danger rapidly enough. The opponents may grasp each other's jaws and spend some time tugging at each other with their jaws locked, but this pattern is much less frequent in *Bettas*, compared to the fighting displays of cichlid fish. Locked jaws do not last long, as both fish must come to the surface every minute or so, to take a gulp of fresh air. *Betta splendens* is an anabantoid and thus must periodically breathe atmospheric oxygen. Both fishes break off their display to take on air. According to the strict code of their ritual, they never attack one another during this necessary interlude. As the fishes tire, the evasive actions become less effective and damage to fins and scales may appear. The gill covers are closed when a serious bite is attempted. Ultimately, and quite suddenly, one of the two fighters loses his splendid colors, folds his fins and darts for a hiding place, with the winner in full pursuit, still nipping at the loser.

The fighting display of the *Betta* is typical of the kind of aggressive interaction that develops between individual fishes. Bettas fight longer and more intensively than other species, but the purpose is the same, the establishment of social rank order and the defense of living space. Fights to the death are rare, but subsequent infections often cause fatalities. Torn fins usually grow in again.

Professional breeders raise bettas in individual glass containers. Photo by Hilmar Hansen.

Bettas displaying.

Cichlids tend to battle jaw to jaw. These are red devils, *Cichlasoma erythraeum*. Photo by Mervin F. Roberts.

Texas cichlids, *Cichlasoma cyanoguttata*, locking jaws.

A dwarf cichlid (*Nanochromis dimidiatus*) has picked a depression under a log as his home. Photo by Hans Joachim Richter.

A pair of blue gouramis, *Trichogaster trichopterus*; the fish in front is the female. Photo by G.J.M. Timmerman.

Dominance and submission

Many studies have been made to identify the factors that determine the winner in a fish battle. Victory does not always go to the stronger, apparently. The most important element seems to be possession of a territory. The resident of a hiding place or the defender of a nest has a definite advantage in combat. Other factors are size, sex, prior experience and events that relate to the actual encounter.

In one study of the establishment of dominance relationships in the blue gourami, *Trichogaster trichopterus*, it was found that two processes could be distinguished: an initial brief phase of status determination and a second, longer period, of status maintenance. The study also suggested that the advantage accruing to resident fish depended primarily on the newcomer's uncertainty and fearfulness in a new situation. As might be expected, relative size differences favored the larger fish, but absolute size. by itself was not a direct factor. Size enters into the prior

experience factor, as larger fish tend to have won more fights in past encounters. A fish that has dominated another one within the last 24 hours had a better chance of winning its bout, whereas a fish that had lost a fight within 24 hours had hardly a chance of winning its battle. This effect was strongest during the 24 hours after a conflict and tended to decrease rapidly for longer intervals.

A mixed population of brown trout *(Salmo trutta)* and rainbow trout *(Salmo gairdneri)* was closely observed in a study carried out in California. They typically took up preferred feeding positions in the stream at places where a constant drift of food particles was available. Except for some of the largest specimens, they defended their position against intruders and established stable hierarchies. Size was the most important element in establishing dominance. A few of the largest individuals were not confined to a particular position and cruised over the whole area. They were non-aggressive and did not attempt to occupy stream positions. Most likely they fed on smaller fishes for which they hunted actively. The rest of the population distributed themselves over the available area. The desirability of a given spot depended on current, the food supply and the availability of cover close by.

It is interesting that despite the fact that these fishes are capable of long-range movements, they voluntarily restrict their activity to a very small portion of their habitat. Once a stable hierarchy has developed, it is very difficult for a transient fish to break into the social structure, as all desirable spots are taken and the group acts as a whole to preserve their relative positions. Only if the top ranking fish is removed is there an opportunity for a subordinate individual to move up. Aggressive behavior is rarely severe, unless the social order is disturbed. Thus, social dominance not only helps to avoid overcrowding, but also to prevent unrestricted aggressiveness and possible injury.

Crowding

Fighting serves the purpose of distributing a group of fishes so as to best utilize the available resources of space and food. Under natural conditions, as well as in a fish tank, the end result is a dynamic equilibrium of a fish population and its environment. Under optimum conditions when food and oxygen supply are abundant, such as in ocean areas where there is an upwelling of food-rich cold water, dense populations of fishes can be supported. Off the coast of Peru, for example, the dense schools of anchovies *(Engraulis ringens)* provide the basis for a thriving fishing industry, as well as for huge nesting colonies of sea birds. Failure of the cold current caused a sudden population crash in 1972 but by spring 1974 the fish were back in full force. The herring and cod fisheries off Newfoundland similarly are based on waters that can support dense schools of these important food fishes.

Typically these aggregations in temper-

A dense school of gray snappers, *Lutjanus griseus*. Photo by Dr. Walter Starck II.

131

A school of fusiliers (*Caesio*) move over a coral reef swarming with anthiids (*Anthias*). Photo by Rodney Jonklaas.

An assembly of tropical reef fishes. Photo by Dr. Gerald Allen.

Male guppies, *Poecilia reticulata*. Guppies do not school; each fish does his own thing. Photo by Dr. Herbert R. Axelrod.

ate and cold waters consist of large numbers of individuals of the same species. In warm and tropical waters, on the other hand, under favorable conditions, such as the presence of coral reefs, there may be a dense fish population, but it will be made up of many different species, each with its own specialized requirements. Tolerance to crowding makes these fishes particularly suitable for home salt water aquariums.

Fish populations expand when conditions are favorable mainly by the successful rearing of their young. Most fishes have a very high reproductive potential, so expansion may be very rapid. An expanding population typically has a preponderance of young individuals. On the other hand, mortality is particularly high in the young. Thus, when conditions are unfavorable the lack of success in breeding and the high death rate of the young results in a population that is relatively old under declining conditions.

One can easily follow the establishment of a population in an aquarium. Start with one pair of guppies *(Poecilia reticulata)*. If they are young fish, the female will still be a virgin and all the subsequent population will descend from this one pair. Aerate the water and feed as much as the fish will consume. Change about two-thirds of the water every week, replacing with water of the same temperature that has been allowed to age for at least 24 hours. Keep count of the fishes, adults and young, each time you change the water. You will find an S-shaped curve of population growth, in other words, first a sharp increase, then a steady rate, finally a levelling off. There will also be a gradual decrease in the average size of fish. This stunting of growth is part of the effect of overcrowding.

Since food and oxygen were not the limiting conditions under this set-up, we must look for behavioral mechanisms. Three major factors have been identified. One is increased cannibalism. The second is heightened aggression, keeping the fish in a continuous highly emotionally aroused state. The third is decreased courtship behavior. In fact only a few of the adult females of the population will succeed in bearing young. These are learned behavior patterns that carry over, even if the available space is increased. For example if a fish population is allowed to stabilize in a large container and its steady population compared with a population that is transferred from a smaller, crowded tank and allowed to reach a steady state over a period of time, it is found that the stable population of the previously crowded group never reaches the same level as that of the comparison group.

Displacement

A very interesting situation develops when a conflict arises between two incompatible behavior tendencies. Frequently, for example, there will be competition between the tendency to advance and the tendency to retreat, when two hostile fishes meet at the borders of their territories. Behavior may be initiated, but not carried through. These behavior patterns are called intention movements. The observer will see incipient aggressive movements, alternating with flight postures. Sometimes, when two incompatible behaviors cannot be carried out, there appears a third, unrelated activity, known as displacement activity.

The three-spined stickleback *(Gasterosteus aculeatus)*, for example, engages in parental fanning during its courtship phase. Parental fanning is appropriate once the eggs are in the nest. The male positions himself in front of the nest and moves his tail as if he wanted to swim forward, while opposing this movement by his pectoral fins. As a result a stream of water moves through the nest, aerating the eggs. In courtship there is a conflict between approach and avoidance of the potential partner. An apparently identical fanning movement can be observed under these circumstances. Since there are no eggs and no nest, this behavior is now inappropriate. As a theoretical explanation, it has been suggested that the conflicting behavior tendencies cancel each other out in such a way that a third behavior pattern can appear instead.

The three-spined stickleback also shows displacement digging when threatened by another male at the edge of his territory. Thus a series of pits may result to mark the boundaries between territories. Cichlid fishes often are also given to displacement digging, many aquarists have discovered to their chagrin, as the end result of this activity is a pitted and unsightly tank with all its plants uprooted and floating at the aquarium surface.

Three-spined stickleback, *Gasterosteus aculeatus.* The aggressive behavior exhibited by this fish is often channeled into displacement digging. Photo by Gunter Senfft.

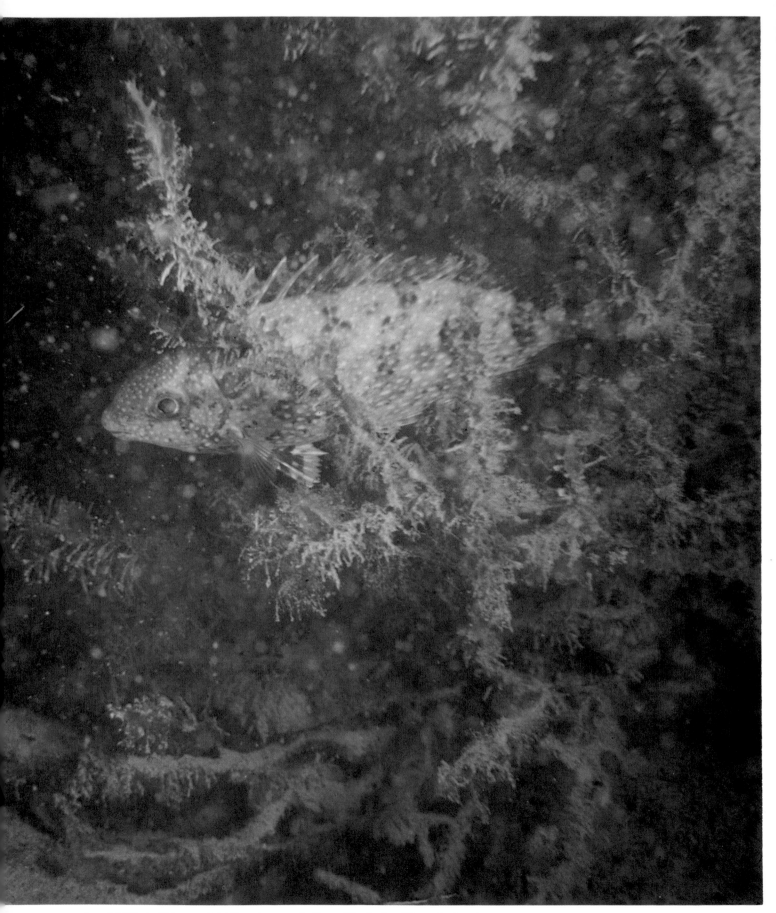

A rabbitfish (*Siganus*) hiding in vegetation. Photo by Pierre Laboute.

Jawfish (*Opistogna-thus aurifrons*) peeking out of its tunnel. Photo by Gerhard Marcuse.

Gold-spotted snake eel, *Myrichthys oculatus*, buried in the sand. Photo by Gerhard Marcuse.

Chapter X

FLEEING AND HIDING

Hiding places

As we have seen, fish behavior is directed toward survival. In fighting between members of the same species the rule is that *"he who fights and runs away, lives to see another day."* Escape from predation is a very serious business in a world where being eaten is a constant danger. A few fishes carry armor or offensive weapons, such as erectile spines, but most shun danger by hiding or by flight. Schooling species rely on presenting a united front. A dense group provides a less desirable target for predators, as it seems to confuse them in some way. Usually it is the straggler or stray that is picked off.

Many fishes hide in natural crevices or caves, where these are available. Coral reefs are a favorite spot, as they provide many hiding places. Anglers know that wrecks and jetties are good for fishing, because fishes tend to hover around these potential hiding places. Freshwater fishes

A grassy area of Lake Malawi, Africa, is used as a hiding place by *Haplochromis* cichlids. Photo by Dr. Herbert R. Axelrod.

A spiny eel, *Mastacembelus armatus*, has emerged from its hiding place. Photo by Dr. Herbert R. Axelrod.

Two spiny eels, *Macrognathus aculeatus*, cross snouts as they stick their heads out of the bottom gravel. Photo by Folke Johnsson.

hide below river banks and in vegetation. Marine flying fishes escape predation by taking to the air, effectively disappearing from the view of their pursuers. A similar capacity is found in the South American hatchet fishes.

Some fishes provide for their own concealment. They bury themselves in the bottom gravel, sand or mud. A number of different and unrelated groups use similar methods. Most of the skates and rays use their wide pectoral fins to stir up the bottom, then let the sand or mud fall back on themselves. The flattened shape of the flounders and their relatives is also well adapted to concealment by burying. These fishes do a good job of hiding themselves by adaptive coloration, but will wriggle their caudal and dorsal fins to bury themselves rapidly in sandy bottom, when the need arises.

The sand lances (Ammodytidae) dive into and out of the sandy bottom with great facility, sometimes remaining buried there while the tide recedes until the return of the next high tide. Clam diggers often uncover them there accidentally. The snake eels (Ophichthidae) hide themselves so quickly in the sand, tail first, that a man digging with a shovel cannot keep up with them. Burrowing head first may be observed in the aquarium in the spiny eel *(Mastacembelus)* and the weatherfish *(Misgurnus)*, actually a member of the loach family (Cobitidae). The jawfishes (Opistognathidae) are well known for their burrowing habits. The activities of these small colorful fishes can be seen easily in a salt-water aquarium. There they use their mouth to excavate tunnels and line them with small stones to prevent cave-ins. Each individual rests diagonally over its hole and will chase off any intruder of its own kind. At the first sign of real or imagined danger they retreat quickly into their refuge.

Still another group of eel-shaped fishes, the garden eels (Heterocongridae), can be found standing upright on their tail above their burrows, ready to dive in, if danger threatens. Their tubes are cemented together with a glue-like substance, secreted

139

The round stingray, *Urolophus jamaicensis*, likes to lie buried in the sand. The venomous stinger at the base of its tail presents a hazard to the unwary. Photo by U. Erich Friese.

Flounders, such as this *Paralichthys olivaceus*, not only bury themselves in the bottom but also are able to match their color pattern to the background. Photo by Dr. Shih-chieh Shen.

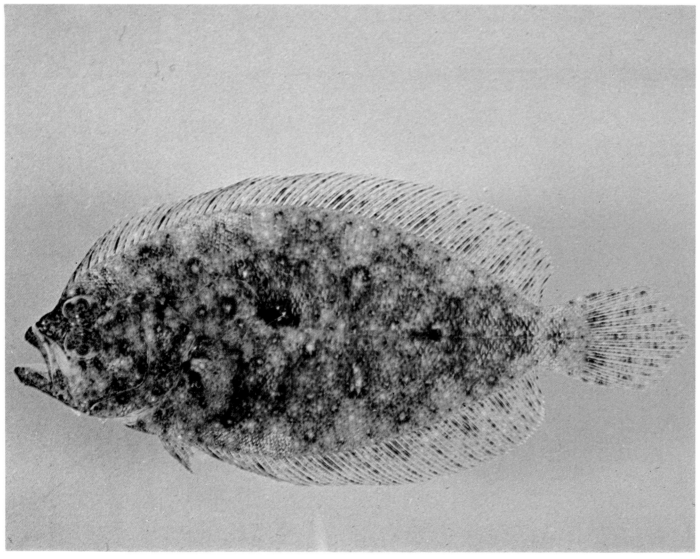

Weatherfishes (*Misgurnus*) frequently bury themselves in the bottom gravel. Photo by Dr. Herbert R. Axelrod.

Damselfish (*Dascyllus albisella*) find their hiding places in coral reefs. Photo by Douglas Faulkner.

Mud minnows excavate and hide in a burrow. This is *Umbra krameri*, a European species. Photo by Karoly Pinter.

A well camouflaged stonefish, *Synanceja verrucosa*, devours two food fish that had come too close to its huge mouth. Photo by Gerhard Marcuse.

by their bodies. A group of them, waving in the water with their heads and bodies look like the sea bottom had grown some strange new crop of stalky plants.

The mudminnows *(Umbra)* constitute another genus of freshwater fishes that excavate and use a burrow for a hiding place. The slippery dick *(Rissola marginata)*, is a member of the blenny-like family Ophidiidae, the cusk eels, most of which live in warm or tropical shores, where they burrow in shallow sandy bottoms. A South African member of this family reaches a length of five feet. These fishes should be distinguished from a group of labroid wrasses that are also called slippery dicks. The habit of the pearlfishes *(Carapus)* of hiding inside the body cavity of a sea cucumber has already been mentioned.

Most aquarists will have noticed that the easiest way to observe the hiding behavior of their fishes is to put a net into their tank in the attempt of catching a particular fish for transfer or examination. A tank that was swarming with fish just a moment ago is suddenly a deserted empty expanse of water as soon as that net is dipped into it. Any fishes that scoot from one corner to another are sure not to be the specimen that is wanted. By an uncanny feat of mind reading, the target fish realizes that he is the one that is to be caught and he isn't about to cooperate!

Protective coloration

Concealment by protective coloration is not necessarily obvious to a human observer, especially one who watches his colorful pets in a lightly planted tank through the pane of an aquarium. Bright colors and patterns of stripes and other markings may be an example of camouflage. Against a proper background of bright coral or thick vegetation these patterns blend into the background and destroy the outline of the body, so that the fishes become practically invisible. It's the same principle that gives the tiger its stripes.

The eye seems to be an especially dangerous give-away. At least that is the explanation offered for the commonly found pattern of a bar through the eye. This pattern destroys the eye's outline and thus confuses the approaching predator. Sometimes an added safety factor is an eye-like spot on the tail or the side of the body, frequently found, for example, in the marine butterfly fishes (Chaetodontidae).

Fishes of the open water cannot rely on this disruptive coloration. They adapt a method of countershading in which the basic color pattern is darker on the back and lighter below. When lighted normally from above, the dark back does not contrast with the darker water, while from below they are inconspicuous against the lighter water surface. An interesting example of an apparent exception to this rule occurs in the upside-down Congo catfish *(Synodontis nigriventris)*, which has a light back and a dark stomach, as indicated by its Latin specific name. The exception is only apparent, however, as this fish prefers to swim with its belly up, searching for food on the underside of leaves and ledges.

Some fishes blend with their background. Coral reef inhabitants are colorful, while reed bed residents wear stripes. Some of the flatfishes are able to change their color pattern to match the background. They become almost invisible when half-buried as well as matched to the gravel or sand bottom. When placed on an artificial pattern, such as a checkerboard design, they will do their best to become checkered, and oddly enough, they are quite successful in doing so.

The most bizarre form of concealment is found in fishes that disguise themselves. The sargassum fish *(Histrio histrio)* resembles a piece of seaweed. It rarely swims freely, but drifts with floating

A sandy area in Lake Malawi, Africa, with its appropriate resident cichlids. Photo by Dr. Herbert R. Axelrod.

The leaf fish, *Monocirrhus polyacanthus*, imitates a floating leaf in its movement, as well as in its appearance. Photo by Harald Schultz.

Butterflyfishes (*Chaetodon auriga*) display a bar to disguise the outline of the real eye and sport a false eye on their dorsal fin. Photo by Dr. Herbert R. Axelrod.

This ghost pipefish, *Solenichthys* sp., easily blends into the seaweed. Photo by Lloyd Grigg.

A splitlure frogfish, *Antennarius scaber*, with its lure extended. It usually lurks in hiding, to pounce on unsuspecting fishes attracted by its lure. A seahorse watches from its perch. Photo by Kurt Severin.

masses of sargassum weed from which it is practically undistinguishable. The leaf fish *(Monocirrhus polyacanthus)* not only looks like a leaf, but has also adopted a leaf-like mode of swimming. It even rests in odd positions which resemble a leaf. Unsuspecting small fishes coming within reach of this apparently drifting dead leaf discover to their peril that there is a gaping mouth attached to one end.

Mimicry

Bright colors and conspicuous patterns often advertise their owner's special characteristics. Thus, poisonous spines or other properties that make a fish inedible may be set off by special patterns. Mimics may imitate these characteristics and benefit from their similarity. This kind of mimicry is well known in insects, but not as commonly found in fishes. One example is the English sole *(Solea vulgaris)*, which imitates the black poisonous spine of the European weever fish *Trachinus*.

Another kind of mimicry has been discovered among the cleaner fishes. These are small, conspicuously colored fishes, often with an horizontal stripe, which pick parasites and bits of dead tissue from the skin, gills and mouths of larger fishes. One such cleaner fish, *Labroides dimidiatus*, a small wrasse, is mimicked by the saber-toothed blenny *Aspidontus taeniatus*. The blenny, almost a perfect imitation of the wrasse, can approach the prospective victim unscathed and bite off small pieces of skin, fins and gills before the surprised host has recognized his mistake. It stands to reason that in this kind of mimicry the number of mimics must always be less than the number of the fish it imitates. Otherwise fishes needing cleaning would start to avoid fishes with the cleaner's pattern, the real cleaners would be out of a job and ultimately the mimics would lose their benefits as well.

Pristigaster cayana, a freshwater clupeid, resembles the shape of the freshwater hatchet-fishes. Photo by Dr. Herbert R. Axelrod.

Parrotfish, *Scarus coelestinus*, hiding in coral reef. Photo by Dr. Walter Starck II.

A labroid wrasse, the slippery dick, *Halichoeres bivittatus*. It advertises rather than conceals its presence. Photo by Dr. John E. Randall.

The upside-down Congo catfish, *Synodontis nigriventris*, prefers to swim with its belly up. Photo by Gene Wolfsheimer.

The sargassum fish, *Histrio histrio*, resembles the drifting seaweed that forms its habitat. Photo by Dr. Herbert R. Axelrod.

The false cleaner, *Aspidontus taeniatus,* (top) mimics the cleaner wrasse, *Labroides dimidiatus,* (bottom) to prey on unsuspecting victims expecting to have their parasites removed. Top photo by Dr. Herbert R. Axelrod, bottom photo by Gerhard Marcuse.

A typical characin, the flame tetra, *Hyphessobrycon flammeus*, scatters its eggs among fine-leaved plants. Photo by Rudolf Zukal.

Copeina guttata, a characin, is unusual in that it spawns occasionally in cichlid fashion in a depression in the sand rather than by scattering its eggs. Photo by Rudolf Zukal.

Chapter XI

COURTSHIP, MATING AND CARE OF YOUNG

Pair formation

As it does in human affairs, sex plays a large role in the life of fishes. There is no uniformity to breeding cycles. Some fishes breed only once in their life, such as the eel or the Pacific salmons, others have specific spawning seasons, one of the best known being the grunion, still others, like the guppy, for example, breed more or less continually.

Great variety exists in the manner of spawning and subsequent care of the young. At one end of the scale are egg scatterers, which release their eggs and pay no further attention to their young after fertilization has taken place. At the other end of the scale are the nest builders, some of whom build elaborate nests and guard their offspring zealously after hatching. Special methods of caring for their eggs have evolved in the case of the mouthbrooders and fishes with egg pouches, such as the sea horse.

In general, egg scatterers produce a greater number of eggs than nest builders, thus assuring survival of sufficient offspring to perpetuate the species despite the great loss of immature individuals. It is of course obvious that the key to avoiding extinction is to assure survival to sexual maturity of sufficient individuals to replace those lost to natural attrition. In the long run, those that do, are successful species, those that don't, become extinct, and those that succeed too well, will eventually suffer from overpopulation and subsequent crowding and starvation. A population in balance with its environment is in a delicate equilibrium and often an apparently minor change in a factor that influences reproduction has far reaching effects on a fish species. It is therefore no wonder that sex related behavior often shows great complexity and has been studied intensively.*

The first step to successful breeding is pair formation. Apparently indiscriminate breeding is found in some species. Spawning is accomplished as the group reaches a high pitch of excitement. Mutual stimulation occurs, but rather than being focused on any individual partner, the group as a whole acts as a breeding community. Herring and mackerel spawn in huge aggregations, scattering eggs and milt freely in the water. *Rasbora heteromorpha* spawn much better in communities, although in the aquarium they can also be bred in pairs or trios. In the case of the *Rasbora*, pairs will break out of the group to deposit eggs on the underside of plant leaves, where a female will extrude her eggs in an upside down position and a male in similar position will immediately fertilize them.

* Readers who are interested in more details than can be found in the survey presented here, should consult C. M. Breder and D. E. Rosen's "Modes of Reproduction in Fishes." Neptune City, N.J., T.F.H. Publications, 1966.

Rasbora heteromorpha deposits its spawn on the underside of broad plant leaves. Photo by Rudolf Zukal.

Fishes that spawn communally have a relatively easy time finding a partner. Other fishes must first go and find a suitable mate. Visual and auditory signals are known to be used for this purpose. Smell and electrosensitivity also play a role, but details have not been well established. A problem that must be overcome in connection with breeding behavior is the social distance normally kept between members of a species.

Close approach is usually equated with aggressive intentions. One of the functions of courtship behavior is to break down the natural reluctance of the female to let the male approach close enough for any sexual union to take place. It might be added that the female's suspicions are well founded. To a human observer, a male *Betta's* courtship appears pretty rugged and by the time the female is ready to spawn, she may be severely

Betta splendens builds a bubble nest. Here the female has just released eggs (upper right), which will be picked up by the male and spit into the nest. Photo by Rudolf Zukal.

A test of strength often precedes cichlid spawning (*Cichlasoma* sp.). Photo by Rudolf Zukal.

roughed up, with her fins in tatters and several scales missing. Cichlid courtship also is often very aggressive. Females are not infrequently killed, if they are not ready to spawn or just unacceptable to the male. On the other hand, if they stand the test of courtship, they form a very stable bond, become a "mated" pair, and will spawn together many times, ignoring all other available partners. Oscars *(Astronotus ocellatus)*, *Pterophyllum*, and *Symphysodon* are well known examples of cichlids that form a very stable and long-lasting, apparently monogamous relationship.

Courtship has several functions in addition to overcoming social distance. Competition between males for available females acts as a selective mechanism, the most vigorous and attractive males being successful in reproduction. The finely tuned interaction of courtship also serves to isolate different species from each other. Especially when closely related species live in the same environment, the different mating displays serve as a barrier to hybridization. This barrier, incidentally, may break down in the aquarium, when no other member of the same species is available for mating. Finally, courtship behavior may help in sex identification in fishes where the sexes are not otherwise differentiated. A male may then distinguish between another male or a female by the way the other fish reacts to his courtship. The distinction that he will have to note, will be the difference between a nip in the fin and a come-hither flip of the tail.

In many fishes where sexes differ in appearance, these differences have a function in courtship. Males, in particular, may put on their best color displays when they go to woo their mates. Many favorite aquarium fishes owe their popularity to their nuptial colors and buyers are often disappointed when their newly introduced acquisitions do not display the beautiful colors seen in illustrations, after these

Female bettas often approach the male during spawning. Photo by Rudolf Zukal.

This female betta has been through a rough courtship. Photo by Rudolf Zukal.

fishes have been safely transported to their homes and added to their fish collection. But if their impatient owners would only wait until their new arrivals have settled down in conditions to their liking, they would be rewarded by colors that often outdo the best that photographer's and printer's skill can provide.

Visual recognition of the readiness to spawn is one of the most widely distributed means of pair formation. Jewel fish *(Hemichromis bimaculatus)* usually are an inconspicuous yellowish green. Both males and females turn a brilliant red, sprinkled with blue, when in a spawning mood. If females are given a choice between a male in courtship color and one that is not, they always spawn on the side of the colorful male. Color, however, is not the only signal. If a male in nuptial colors is blinded with eye cups, it will lack normal movements; the female will now pick an active plain male in preference to a highly colored, but inactive male.

Sound as a signal of readiness to mate is probably common, but not as well established as visual signaling, due to the difficulties in making these sounds audible to the human ear. "Mating calls" have been found in a characin, *Glandulocauda inequalis*, the croaking gourami, *Trichopsis (=Ctenops) vittatus*, the cichlid *Tilapia mossambica*, and some cyprinids, such as the satinfin shiner *Notropis analostanus*. Among salt water fishes, examples include the toadfish, *Opsanus tau*, the goby, *Bathygobius soporator*, some blennies, various croakers and drums (Sciaenidae), sea robins *(Prionotus)*, seahorses *(Hippocampus)* and various damselfishes *(Eupomacentrus)*. In a study of the bicolor damselfish *(Eupomacentrus partitus)*, sound was recorded in the ocean near Bimini in the Bahamas. Various sounds were heard during courtship. These were called chirps, grunts and pops by the investigators. When played back in an aquarium, chirps and grunts put males in a courtship mood, as indicated

Spawning fishes often display nuptial colors. (Top) Jewel-fish, *Hemichromis bimaculatus*, and (bottom) rosy barbs (*Puntius conchonius*) long-finned variety. Top photo by Rudolf Zukal, bottom photo by Hans Joachim Richter.

The male of the blenny species *Blennius pavo* secretes a chemical sex attractant. Photo by Stanislav Frank.

Three-spined stickleback, *Gasterosteus aculeatus*. Only the male (lower fish) changes color. Female is heavy with eggs. Photo by Stanislav Frank.

A male guppy, *Poecilia reticulata,* displays to the female (see p. 159). Photo by Rudolf Zukal.

The male shubunkin (goldfish variety), *Carassius auratus,* displays sex tubercles on his gill covers (operculum) during the breeding season. Photo by Laurence Perkins.

by their behavior and color changes, whereas the pop was found to inhibit courtship.* Aquarium fanciers with sophisticated sound recording and playback facilities might well make a contribution to science by listening to their fishes' courtship. As far as is known, no fish has ever been heard to object to being "bugged."

It would be surprising if senses other than sight and hearing did not also play a role in pair formation, but not too much is known about them at the present time. The male blenny, *Blennius pavo*, secretes an attractant from a gland that arouses the female. The female goby, *Bathygobius soporator*, on the other hand, exudes a scent that starts courtship behavior in the male. The shad *(Alosa alosa)* and the bullhead *(Ictalurus nebulosus)* have also been found to respond to olfactory stimulation. Tactile stimulation plays a large part in courtship, but undoubtedly also comes into the picture in pair recognition. Our understanding of the functions of electrical sensitivity is still rudimentary, both for the strongly electrical fishes, such as the electric eel *(Electrophorus electricus)* and the electric catfish *(Malapterurus electricus)*, and the weakly electric fishes, such as the gymnotids, the mormyrids and *Gymnarchus*. Suggestive evidence for electrical signals in courtship has, thus far, been claimed for the electric eel and the mormyrids, but it would not be unlikely, if all made use of their capabilities.

Display

Once a pair has been formed there follows a more or less fixed sequence of displays that serves a twofold purpose. It binds the partners together, as they follow the typical steps of courtship procedure.

* For a full description of this study, see A. A. Myrberg, Jr., Ethology of the bicolor damselfish, *Eupomacentrus partitus* (Pisces: Pomacentridae): A comparative analysis of laboratory and field behavior. *Animal Behaviour Monographs*, 1972, 5, 197–283.

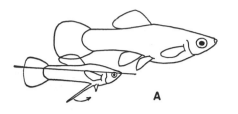
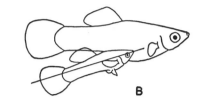
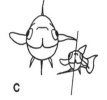
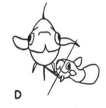
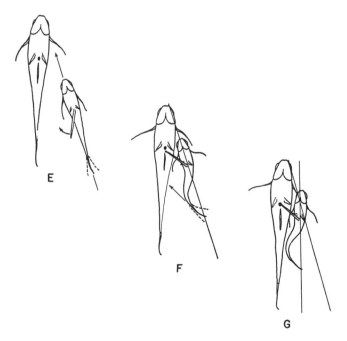

Guppies display in a manner that is typical of livebearers. (A) Male approaches from behind and slightly below the female. (B) He swings his gonopodium forward. (C) The male thrusts and (D) makes contact with the female. (E), (F), and (G) present a view of the same sequence as seen from below.

Albino paradise fish, *Macropodus opercularis*, in courtship. Photo by Jaroslav Elias.

Albino paradise fish, *Macropodus opercularis*, beginning their nuptial embrace. Photo by Jaroslav Elias.

The paradise fish sink slowly to the bottom as the female is almost ready to extrude her eggs. Photo by Jaroslav Elias.

In addition, courtship display serves to arouse the fishes sexually and thus to initiate the physiological changes that are necessary to successful mating. These include the secretion of endocrine glands, particularly the pituitary, as well as ovulation and extrusion of the ovipositor tube in the female and the swelling of the genital papilla in the male.

The three-spined stickleback *(Gasterosteus aculeatus)* has been studied extensively. The male is territorial and builds his nest before courtship starts. When he spots a ripe female, a typical behavior sequence develops. The male pursues the female in a zig-zag pattern. If ready, she displays to the male, who leads her to the nest. If she follows, he then shows her the nest entrance, which she enters. The male then butts the female's protruding tail, while she deposits her eggs. As she leaves the nest, he enters and fertilizes the eggs. Variations of the pattern are possible and often there is a repetition of a particular step in the display, but the essential elements are fixed and typical of the courtship of a particular species.

As an example of a livebearer, we will describe the display of the guppy *(Poecilia reticulata)*. These fish are non-territorial and promiscuous. The male will display to any female, but is more attracted by a

Male three-spined stickleback, *Gasterosteus aculeatus,* enters nest. Photo by Gunter Senfft.

Male three-spine stickleback leaving nest after fertilizing eggs. Photo by Gunter Senfft.

larger female than by a smaller one. He attempts to attract the female's attention by swimming back and forth in front of her, intensifying his color patterns and spreading his fins and tail. Should the female show some interest, the male increases his efforts. He attempts to isolate the female from her group, confine her to a particular spot and performs a typical movement in which the body is S-shaped, tail fins are folded and very rapid shaking movements take place. If the female is uninterested, she pays no attention to all this effort, but if she is cooperative, she approaches by propelling herself toward the male by a movement of the pectoral and caudal fins, in contrast to the normal swimming movement involving the whole body. The male attempts to get behind and slightly below the female, at the same time swinging forward his gonopodium, the modified anal fin, which serves as the intromittent organ in livebearers. Although

male guppy displays are very frequent, actual fertilization demands the cooperation of the female and is relatively rare. Most of the thrusting movements of the male are unsuccessful, even if the tip of the gonopodium momentarily touches the genital area of the female. A receptive female arches her body slightly. The male thrusts and the tip of his gonopodium makes contact with the female for several seconds. The tip of the gonopodium has a tiny hook, which engages the female in a successful mating. Guppies are right or left handed in the preferred side from which they approach the female. The pelvic fin on the side toward the female moves forward to support the gonopodium during insemination. The fishes wheel in a tight circle while in contact. After insemination the male jumps away and performs a series of jerky movements. The female, on the other hand, swims away in a distinctly nonchalant manner.

Dwarf gouramis, *Colisa lalia,* build bits of plant life into their bubble nest. Photo by Rudolf Zukal.

Paradise fish build their nest of air bubbles coated with saliva. Photo by Jaroslav Elias.

Although an anabantoid, *Betta brederi* is a mouthbreeder. The male incubates the eggs in his mouth. Photo by E. Roloff.

Ctenopoma maculata has no need to build a bubble nest, as the eggs float. Photo by Hans Joachim Richter.

Male guppy, showing gonopodium swung forward. American Museum of Natural History photo.

A partially demolished three-spined stickleback nest showing the eggs.

Nest building

If pair formation corresponds to falling in love and display to courting, then nest building is the equivalent of house hunting in the world of fishes. Of course there are many fishes that do not build a nest in the sense of a well-defined structure. A number of them, however, will spend some time in preparing a natural spawning site.

Among nest builders the most elaborate structures, comparable to the nest of birds, are found among the sticklebacks (Gasterosteidae). The three-spined stickleback *(Gasterosteus aculeatus)* in early spring ascends fresh water streams from the coastal regions where it has spent the winter. When it has found a suitable spot, it takes on breeding colors, a brilliant red belly in the male, and, of paramount importance with respect to nest building, develops a special glue-secreting gland in the kidney. Readiness to build depends on the presence of appropriate plant material. Several males kept in a bare aquarium, for example, will not change

Ovipositor of *Aequidens pulcher*, the blue acara, showing egg being extruded (see pp. 173-174). Photo by Kassanyi Jeno.

color or establish territories. Add some plants in a corner of the tank, and one of the males will change color, start defending its territory and begin nest building. It digs a shallow depression in the sand, then methodically sets about collecting small bits of plant life which it arranges into a tubular nest by gluing them together with the sticky, insoluble secretion of its kidney gland. A hole is left through the middle of the structure for the female to enter and the male to follow, as described in the previous section.

Related species of stickleback modify their nest building pattern somewhat. For example, the four-spined stickleback *(Apeltes quadracus)* weaves his walnut-sized, round nest among the stems of water plants. There are many sticklebacks, with spines ranging from two to 15 and more, each species with its own typical nest.

A different kind of nest, not quite as elaborate as the stickleback's, is the bubble nest built by many of the anabantoids, such as the Siamese fighting fish *(Betta splendens),* the croaking gouramis, genus *Trichopsis (=Ctenops),* the blue gourami *(Trichogaster trichopterus)* and the paradise fish *(Macropodus opercularis).* All build their nests essentially by the same method. A bubble of air is swallowed at the water surface, coated with mucus and carefully spit out at the spot selected for a nest. Usually this location provides protection and some support, such as some floating plants or a corner of an aquarium. The bubbles pile up above the surface of the water to form a mound. Eggs are placed between the bubbles and newly hatched young remain in the nest until free swimming. Some species, for example the dwarf gourami *(Colisa lalia),* prefer to weave bits of plant life into the bubble nest. Other, like the kissing gourami *(Helostoma temminckii),* build a very perfunctory nest, which soon falls apart, but this does not harm the eggs, as they float by themselves. Some of the anabantoids that do not build

a bubble nest also have free-floating eggs, for example, *Ctenopoma oxyrhynchus;* others are mouthbreeders, such as the chocolate gourami *(Sphaerichthys osphromenoides)* and Breder's betta *(Betta brederi).* Bubble nests are not confined to anabantoids; the armored catfish *Callichthys callichthys* is also a bubble nest builder.

In most cases the male does the nest building by himself, chasing away any female that comes near the nest site. In fact, the anabantoid males tend to treat their females so notoriously roughly, that it is a good idea to separate the sexes by a glass pane inserted into the aquarium until

Dwarf gourami *(Colisa)* bubble nest.

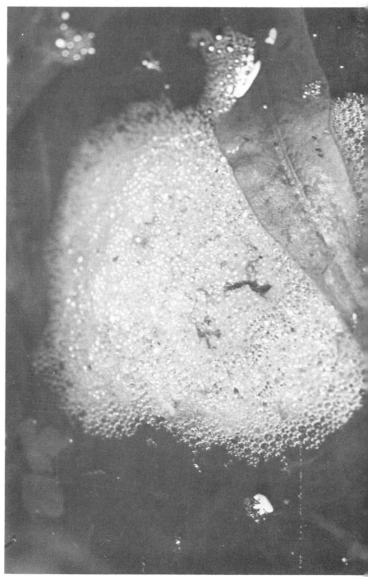

Ctenopoma maculata coming out of nuptial embrace. Each egg contains a small oil droplet to make it float. Photo by Hans Joachim Richter.

The chocolate gourami, *Sphaerichthys osphromenoides*, had breeders mystified for a long time. (Top) A pair in embrace. (Bottom) The eggs are extruded. (Contd. p. 172). Photos by Hans Joachim Richter.

The male blue gourami, *Trichogaster trichopterus*, (shown here) normally builds the bubble nest and takes care of the young, but the females also are potentially capable of parental behavior, specially under the influence of male sex hormone. Photo by Gerhard Budich.

the nest is ready. The females themselves may be quite eager to help, however. The author remembers a little female *Betta* that got her way. The gorgeous male had practically killed his first mate, so a glass partition was inserted, reaching about an inch above the water surface, and a new female provided on the other side. Returning to check the tank after a while, I was unable to see the female in her compartment. To our surprise, two fishes were building the bubble nest. The male was not too happy about his helpmate, but the female was busy adding her own bubbles to the rising mound. How had she managed to get through the barrier? The mystery was soon solved. The female was netted and returned to her compartment. In typical *Betta* fashion, she accepted the situation, without showing obvious fright or disturbance. About a minute or two later she swam to the partition, arched her body and with a graceful leap cleared the barrier to rejoin her mate. Although it is rare for *Betta* females to help in nest building, it is more frequent in dwarf gourami *(Colisa lalia)* couples. It should also be noted that in anabantoids as well as in cichlids there is a necessity for compatibility between pairs; some couples do not seem to "hit it off" under any circumstances. Males may accept or reject certain females for no apparent reasons, and females also seem to have the ability to choose which male they will accept for mating.

Studies have shown that nest building and parental behavior are under the influence of the male sex hormones, the androgens. In one experiment, the species tested, the blue gourami, *Trichogaster trichopterus*, is considered to be one in which the male normally builds the nest and takes care of the eggs. One of the tasks used as a test was egg retrieval, a normal component of parental behavior. Males, as expected, retrieved eggs much more frequently than females, but, in connection with the previous discussion, it is interesting to note that some females also acted in this way. Of 14 males and 15 females, all the males retrieved within five minutes, but only four females retrieved during the first five minutes, and two more were seen to do so later. Only one female retrieved as frequently as was normal for males. Male sex hormone (testosterone) pellets were now implanted in seven females, eight others receiving an implant of cholesterol as a control. None of the control group built nests, five of the seven testosterone treated females did.

The experimentally treated females retrieved significantly more eggs than the control group and also showed a greater degree of other parental behavior. We cannot say that the androgens caused the parental behavior. But we can claim that the results indicate a greater tendency for male parental behavior in the female when exposed to appropriate conditions. Some females are responsive to eggs under normal conditions, but this tendency is enhanced when the male hormone level is raised. The potentiality for this behavior is present in both sexes.

Similar findings have been reported in both the dwarf gourami *(Colisa lalia)* and the paradise fish *(Macropodus opercularis)* when females were treated with

The croaking gourami, *Trichopsis vittatus*, prefers a broad-leaved plant as the location of its bubble nest. Photo by Rudolf Zukal.

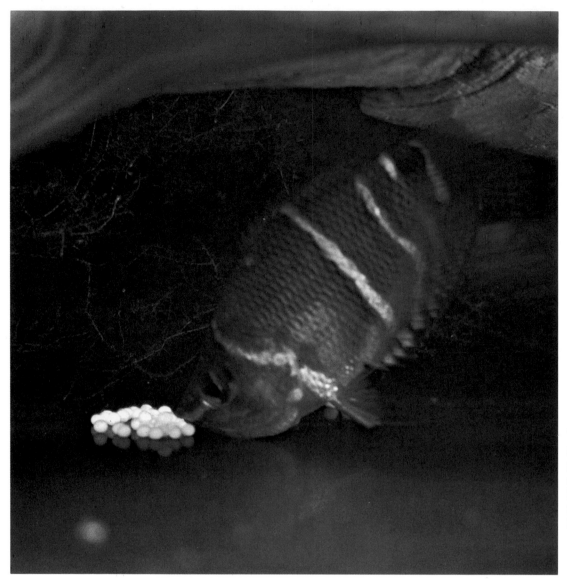

The chocolate gourami now picks up the eggs for incubation in a most ungourami-like action.

With eggs safely cradled in its mouth, the fish moves toward the surface for a gulp of air. Photos by Hans Joachim Richter.

A blue acara (*Aequidens pulcher*) pair in preliminary test of strength (top), guarding the spawn (middle) and the fry (bottom). Top photo by Dr. Herbert R. Axelrod, middle photo by Rudolf Zukal and bottom photo by Kassanyi Jeno.

male sex hormones. Other species in which the male builds a nest have also been shown to be influenced by androgens. These include the three-spined stickleback *(Gasterosteus aculeatus)* and two species of sunfish, the pumpkinseed *(Lepomis gibbosus)* and the longeared sunfish *(Lepomis megalotis)*. Both sexes participate in nest building (not a bubble nest, though) in the cichlid *Tilapia macrocephala*, although the female builds more than the male. Castration does not appear to affect the male pattern of behavior, but ovariectomy reduced female nest building to the low level of the male. Finally, it might be noted that our notion that care of the young is a female characteristic is contradicted by these experiments, which clearly show that the sex·role assignment

is a matter of evolutionary development and, in fishes at least, is largely affected by internal states.

A depression dug in the sand or gravel bottom of a river, a lake or an aquarium frequently serves as a nest in a pattern common to a wide range of species. Many of the cichlids clean off a depression until they reach a solid surface, a rock or the bottom slate of an aquarium, on which they deposit their eggs. The blue acara *(Aequidens pulcher)* can serve as a typical example. Preliminary to spawning there is a test of strength, involving a great deal of aggressive behavior, particularly a tug-of-war in which the fishes grab each other by the jaw and try to dislodge each other. After the young are hatched, they are frequently transferred to new nests built

Blue acaras typically dig a depression in the sand until a hard surface is found. Photo by Rudolf Zukal.

During a tug-of-war the blue acara engages the horny outer surfaces of the lips and rarely causes damage. Photo by Kassanyi Jeno.

in depressions in the sand. Both parents participate in this care-giving behavior. An interesting aspect of this activity has been discussed in connection with the nest-building behavior of the West African cichlid *Tilapia mariae*. The pair bond established in the prespawning display can be tested by confining one partner behind a glass partition and observing the behavior of the other partner. If a pair bond has been established, the second fish will stay close to the glass, otherwise it will swim about freely. After spawning it was found that the parents avoid each other, their association is now kept up only by their mutual interest in their offspring, which may be moved several times by both parents. When the young are old enough to go out on their own, a new breeding cycle commences and the pair is reunited.

Among other well known nest builders are the sunfishes (Centrarchidae), including not only the sunfishes proper *(Lepomis)*, but also the largemouth and smallmouth bass *(Micropterus)* and the rock bass

(Ambloplites) and relatives. They nest in a round depression in sand or gravel, which is carefully swept out and cleaned before spawning commences. An excavation under a rock serves as a nest for many other fishes. The eggs are attached to the roof of the resulting cave-like structure, the parents spawning in upside down position. Examples are the various dwarf cichlids, genera *Nannacara, Pelvicachromis*, Johnny darter *(Etheostoma nigrum)*, the stream-dwelling sculpins *(Cottus)* and the blunt-nose and fathead minnows *(Pimephales)*. A tunnel is dug and serves as a nest site for some of the catfishes, such as the channel catfish, *Ictalurus punctatus* and the whiptail *Loricaria*.

Nesting in holes of coral reefs or in abandoned conch shells is typical of the demoiselles, such as the sergeant major *(Abudefduf saxatilis)* and the beau gregory *(Pomacentrus leucostictus)*. The pomacentrid *Abudefduf zonatus* lives in the inner reef of coral islands. Males are territorial and promiscuous. In other words, no permanent pair bond is formed. Males

Whiptail loricaria, *Loricaria filamentosa,* nesting in hollow bamboo section. Both parents clean the spawning site. The male assumes care of the eggs. Photo by Rudolf Zukal.

Marine fishes are seldom observed on their nest. (Top) An anemonefish, *Amphiprion perideraion*, shelters its eggs next to the protection of its anemone. (Bottom) Pomacentrid (*Abudefduf*) tending its nest. These fishes are usually described as nesting in coral or empty conch shells, but this individual seems to have picked the pilings of an abandoned wharf. Upper photo by Dr. Gerald Allen, bottom photo by Dr. Herbert R. Axelrod.

A North American sunfish, the pumpkinseed, *Lepomis gibbosus*. Pumpkinseeds' nests, depressions cleaned of all debris on the bottom of shallow lakes or slow moving rivers, can easily be spotted during the spawning season. Photo by Chvojka Milan.

The beau gregory, *Pomacentrus leucostictus*, excavates a nest centered on an empty clam shell.

The brown trout, *Salmo trutta*, is one of the widely distributed food fishes in the world. There are many variants of the species often considered as subspecies that are either migratory, non-migratory or both. Photo by Miloslav Kocar.

excavate a nest centered on an empty clam shell. Digging first with their body, they clear the shell of sand until it sits in the center of a circular depression. They then clean out the interior of the clam shell, using their mouth to pick up coral fragments, carrying them away and spitting them out at some distance from the nest site. An attempt is made to move larger coral pieces by pushing them with the open mouth. Females have territories dispersed among the males. Courtship starts when a male suddenly puts on his conspicuous breeding pattern and enters one of the female's territories. Mating takes place inside the clam shell and the eggs are deposited at one of its ends. Only the males guard and take care of the eggs. The absence of pair bonding correlates nicely with what was said before with regard to *Tilapia mariae*. The nest building and spawning behavior of cichlids (Cichlidae) and damselfishes (Pomacentridae) has been considered sufficiently similar to indicate a close systematic relationship.

Recently, however, taxonomists have found behavioral differences that make this relationship doubtful. The North American sunfishes (Centrarchidae), also with similar breeding patterns, may be closely related to the pomacentrids, however.

All the nest building species considered so far share the characteristic of taking care of their eggs and young. The salmon and trout family (Salmonidae) is an example of fishes that build a nest, but do not pay any further attention to it after spawning. The nest is excavated in the riffles of fast moving streams. The streambed must be a suitable combination of sand and gravel. Once chosen, territories are formed and defended. Excavation is carried out by body flexion. The body movements stir up the stones and sand of the bottom of the stream. The fast moving water sweeps them downstream before they can settle again. Repetition of this action eventually results in a cleared area of gravel, terminating downstream in a mound of finer gravel and sand. The shape

Tilapia mariae is a substrate spawning member of the genus (see p. 175). The parents share in guarding the eggs (top). They dig a depression in the sand to confine the wriggling mass of newly hatched young (middle). The fry have just began to swim (bottom).

The cloud of youngsters becomes less dense as they mature and become more adventurous (top). The eight-week-old young assume the barred color pattern of the juvenile (middle). The young are ready to take up life of their own, and the parents are now showing renewed interest in each other preparatory to the next spawning. Photos by Gerhard Marcuse.

of the nest depends on the speed of water flow; it is round in slower flowing portions of the stream and elongated in faster moving waters. During spawning the adhesive eggs fall between the small stones of the gravel bed, where the nest structure prevents them from being swept away by the current. As soon as the eggs are deposited and fertilized, the nest is deserted and the next nest excavated slightly upstream. Fine sand and small stones from this new nest drift over and into the old nest, covering and protecting the eggs. The cycle of nest building and spawning continues until the fishes are exhausted. Atlantic salmon *(Salmo salar)* return to the ocean after spawning, but the Pacific salmons *(Oncorhynchus)* breed only once and then die.

Tiger or Sumatra barbs *(Capoeta tetrazona)* spawning. Most of the adhesive eggs fall onto the plants. Photo by Rudolf Zukal.

Spawning

Most species of fish do not build a nest at all, and pay no further attention to their eggs after spawning, except perhaps for eating them. Spawning, however, is by no means indiscriminate. Very specific conditions of temperature, pH, water hardness, light and dark and the presence of appropriate plants and bottom covering may be decisive factors in inducing spawning.

Typically, spawning is preceded by a period during which the male actively pursues the female. Exceptions occur in some cases. The Sumatra barb *(Capoeta tetrazona)* female often starts off courtship by chasing the male. The head and tail light, *Hemigrammus ocellifer,* also often has the female initiating the pursuit. In the end, however, the male takes over and drives the female until, typically, the pair comes together side by side, the female expels her eggs with a quivering motion, and the male immediately fertilizes them. Non-adhesive eggs, such as those of the zebra fish *(Brachydanio rerio)* fall to the bottom and lodge between stones. Adhesive eggs are scattered over plants, where they stick fast, by many favorite aquarium fishes, such as most characins (Characidae) and barbs *(Puntius)*. The South American armored catfishes of the genus *Corydoras* lay adhesive eggs which the female clasps in her ventral fins and deposits on a leaf or other spawning site.

Among the cyprinodonts of the genera *Cynolebias, Aphyosemion, Nothobranchius* and *Pterolebias* and their relatives, two kinds of spawning take place. The surface spawners scatter their eggs among floating plants. Contrary to the species discussed before, spawning is stretched out over a period of days and subsequent hatching of the young also takes much longer than in the previously mentioned fishes. The second type, known as bottom spawners, bury their eggs in the ground. Both parents dive into the soft bottom layer, usually well-boiled peat moss in aquarium

A bottom-spawning cyprinodont, *Cynolebias whitei*, shown here diving into the substrate. Photo by Chvojka Milan.

culture, to deposit their eggs. Hatching is facilitated by a period of semi-drying. After return to the water the eggs hatch within 24 hours. The time interval between egg laying and hatching may be two to three weeks or as long as seven to nine months. This method of spawning has been adopted by these so-called annual breeders to overcome the problem of survival in small lakes and ditches that are subject to drying up during seasonal droughts. The parents die, but the next generation hatches and grows to maturity very quickly. These fishes occur in tropical and subtropical waters throughout the world, in West Africa *(Aphyosemion)*, in East Africa *(Nothobranchius)*, in northern South America *(Pterolebias* and *Austrofundulus myersi)* and in Argentina and southeastern Brazil *(Cynolebias* and *Cyno-*

poecilus). In some instances it has been observed that some of these fishes can spawn either at the surface or in the bottom layer, for example, *Aphyosemion bivittatum* and *Cynopoecilus melanotaenia*.

A variation of the adhesive egg laying technique occurs in a number of species in which the female carries the eggs around with her on a tough string after fertilization. The best known example is the Japanese rice fish, the medaka, *Oryzias latipes*. The cluster of eggs eventually attaches itself to some floating plants, a leaf or a twig, when the female accidentally swims close to it. In addition to *Oryzias*, this breeding habit is known in the Cuban minnow, *Cubanichthys cubensis*, in the yellow finned lampeye, *Aplocheilichthys flavipinnis* and other *Oryzias* and some *Rivulus* species.

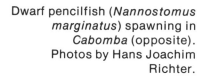

Dwarf pencilfish (*Nannostomus marginatus*) spawning in *Cabomba* (opposite). Photos by Hans Joachim Richter.

Nothobranchius rachovi is a bottom-spawning annual fish. Photos by Hans Joachim Richter.

Oryzias javanicus, the Javanese rice fish, carries her eggs, attached by a tough string to her vent, until the string is accidentally snagged and the eggs come to rest on a plant. Photo by A. Van Den Nieuwenhuizen.

We have previously mentioned some fishes with parasitic feeding habits. The bitterling *(Rhodeus sericeus)* is not truly parasitic in its breeding habits, but its method of reproduction does represent a severe imposition on the host. At breeding time the female bitterling develops a long ovipositor tube which she inserts into a fresh water mussel to deposit her eggs. The male sheds his sperm in the general vicinity at the same time, where they are drawn into the mussel's gill chamber to fertilize the eggs by the mussel's normal breathing cycle. The young hatch and spend the period until they are free-swimming in the gill chamber, without, apparently, inconveniencing the mussel sufficiently to cause any ill effects. The bitterling was introduced to the United States about 1925 and there was some question whether it would find a suitable equivalent of the European fresh water mussel it used for spawning purposes. As it turned out, at least two kinds of mussel were suitable. A Japanese relative *(Acheilognathus)* also incubates its eggs in a mussel. In a parallel manner, the un-related lumpsucker *(Caraproctus)* uses the carapace of the Kamchatka crab as an incubator. In the case of still another unrelated fish, the tubesnout *Aulichthys japonicus*, the eggs are laid in the peribranchial cavity of the ascidian *Cynthia roretzi*.

We are used to thinking of fishes as being bound to their watery environment, but some, like the walking catfish *(Clarias)* occasionally move overland, and others, like some *Rivulus* species, for example, *Rivulus harti*, often are found clinging to vegetation at the water's edge, or the glass sides or cover of an aquarium above the water line. They may spend some time there, before dropping back into the water. But there is only one species that deposits its eggs outside the water. The jumping characin, *Copeina arnoldi*, is unique in its spawning habit. In nature it will use an overhanging leaf, or, in the aquarium, the glass wall or some other site provided by the breeder. A pair will leap from the water to the site it has selected and cling to it long enough for the female to deposit some eggs and for the male to fertilize them. This process is repeated until an egg mass of about a hundred eggs is deposited. The male now takes up a station below the eggs and keeps them moist by splashing water on them periodic-ally for the three days it takes them to hatch, when the young fall back into the water. Actually the father probably cannot see his eggs, but remembers their location by observing the lower edge of the spawning site, which he then uses as a target. When eggs were removed from a circular disk that has been used for spawning and another identical target provided, the male kept up his splashing for about three days. It was shown that the male used the spawning disk as his target, rather than some underwater landmark, by the observation that he moved his station, if the disk was moved sideways. The lower edge appeared to be used for aiming, as demonstrated by the point hit by the splash, if a larger or smaller disk was substituted for the original size.

Protecting the young

Care of the young is well developed in some of the nest building species, but reaches its height in fishes that have one of the parents carrying eggs and newly hatched young either in their mouth or in a pouch. Oral incubation has evolved in many different groups of fishes. Best known to aquarists are the mouthbreeding cichlids, such as various *Tilapia*, *Geophagus*, and *Haplochromis* species. Less well

A female bitterling, *Rhodeus sericeus*, about to deposit her eggs into a mussel's exhalant siphon. Photo by Laurence Perkins.

Spawning of the armored catfish, *Corydoras aeneus*. Male courting female. Photo by Rudolf Zukal.

A female clasping eggs in her pelvic fins. Photo by Rudolf Zukal.

Eggs are attached individually to plant leaves and stems or the aquarium sides. Photo by Rudolf Zukal.

The eggs are large and adhesive. Photo by Rudolf Zukal.

Three males and one female (middle fish of group on the right) in a bare tank are a typical breeding set-up. These are albino *Corydoras aeneus*. Photo by Giancarlo Padovani.

known are various anabantids, such as the painted betta, *Betta picta*, and the chocolate gourami, *Sphaerichthys osphromenoides*, which have abandoned bubble nests for oral care of their eggs and young. Other oral incubators are found among the arapaimas (Osteoglossidae), the jawfishes (Opistognathidae), marine catfish of the Ariidae family and the marine cardinal fishes (Apogonidae).

The male marine gafftopsail catfish *(Bagre marinus)*, although only about two feet in length, carries up to 55 large eggs, the size of marbles, in his mouth. In common with most mouthbreeders, he does not eat during his "pregnancy" and consequently becomes very emaciated. The male also serves as a living incubator in the sea catfish *Galeichthys felis*, whereas

both male or female may carry the eggs in the marine cardinal fishes (Apogonidae) of tropical waters, which sometimes carry more than a hundred eggs, bound together in a package by adhesive threads.

In numerous African cichlids of the genus *Haplochromis*, the female incubates the eggs. The male starts the spawning pattern by digging a shallow pit, much like that of other bottom spawning cichlids. He coaxes the female to the depression where she lays her eggs and almost immediately picks them up in her mouth. In some *Haplochromis* males, for example *Haplochromis wingati* and *H. burtoni*, there are conspicuous egg-like spots on the anal fin of the male. One hypothesis has it that these spots serve as a substitute for eggs. According to this theory, the

Haplochromis wingati male with egg-like spots on the anal fin. Photo by Gerhard Marcuse.

eggs have not been fertilized by the time the female has picked them up. By pecking at the imitation eggs, the female inhales the sperm which the male releases at this time. It would seem more research is needed to confirm this hypothesis, as it seems strange that so many other related fishes manage so well without these spots.*

Tilapia never have egg-spots, but in *Tilapia macrochir* another mechanism has been discovered that may have evolved to aid fertilization. The female serves as incubator. She picks up the unfertilized eggs in her mouth. The male produces filament-like spermatophores which the female picks up if she finds them. The males possess long, filament-like spermatophore models that protrude from their genital region. The females pick at these attachments with their mouth, thus making sure that they also take up the real spermatophores which are interspersed with the dummies.

The South American cichlids of the genus *Geophagus* and the African mbunas and *Tilapia* are made up of some species in which the male incubates, others in which the female incubates and still others in which spawning occurs on the bottom without oral incubation. It may well be that we are catching here a glimpse of evolution in progress. If, for example, breeding takes place in an environment, such as a lake shore with fluctuating water level, where the nest and eggs may be destroyed by the receding lake water, the mouthbreeder is obviously better off, as he can carry his offspring with him in an emergency. Thus mouthbreeding confers a selective advantage over its alternatives and a tendency will develop for mouth-

* H. R. Axelrod offers an alternate hypothesis, based on his personal experience while diving in Lakes Malawi and Tanganyika, that the "egg spots" serve the purpose of identification in the dark and murky depths where these fishes are found. A complete discussion and many beautiful illustrations may be found in: H. R. Axelrod, African cichlids of Lakes Malawi and Tanganyika, second ed., Neptune City, N.J.: T.F.H. Publications, 1974, pp. 31 ff.

Copeina arnoldi, the jumping characin, showing eggs deposited on sanded glass above waterline.

Young gaff-topsail catfish, *Bagre marinus*. These fish have not yet absorbed their yolk sacs and would normally be carried in the mouth of the incubating male. American Museum of Natural History photo.

A pair of *Pelvicachromis taeniatus* seriously guarding their young. Fish in the foreground is the male. Photo by Hans Joachim Richter.

The inside of a halved coconut shell has been picked as a spawning site by this dwarf cichlid, *Apistogramma wickleri*. Note unusual red color of eggs. Photo by Hans Joachim Richter.

A julie, *Julidochromis ornatus,* has spawned on the side of a rock. These cichlids are endemic to the hard, alkaline waters of Lake Tanganyika. Photo by Hans Joachim Richter.

brooders to increase at the expense of their rivals.

Complex behavior changes are related to the capability to incubate orally. For example, the usual cichlid mode of fighting, where a pair catches each other by the jaw and conducts a tug of war, is replaced in mouthbreeders by a pushing and shoving match. The key to successful incubation is the inhibition of egg swallowing. In experiments on the black-chinned mouthbreeder, *Tilapia melanotheron*, it was shown that immature fish and mature fish without spawning experience treated eggs as a

The possible ways in which the young are protected are by no means exhausted by the examples given thus far. Females of the obstetrical catfish (Aspredinidae) carry their eggs attached to their belly by little stalks. In the North American blind cave fishes (Amblyopsidae) the female carries the eggs in her gill chamber. Males do their share too. The humphead males (Kurtidae) carry their eggs in a cluster attached to a hook on their forehead. A South American catfish, *Loricaria typus*, carries his eggs in a pouch formed by an enlarged lower lip. Best known are the

Freshwater pipefish (*Syngnathus spicifer*). The female deposits her eggs into the male's brood pouch (see p. 195). Photo by A. Van den Nieuwenhuizen.

welcome addition to their diet and swallowed them immediately. Fish that had spawned at least once, but not immediately prior to the experiment, showed some deficit in picking up eggs. It appears that the spawning process itself plays an important role in getting the fish ready to incubate. The fish readily distinguish unfertilized eggs, saline soaked eggs and artificial eggs from normal eggs. Even when blinded or made incapable of smelling, pairs of fish picked up eggs normally, apparently compensating for their sensory loss.

seahorses *(Hippocampus)* and their relatives, the pipefishes *(Syngnathus)*, in which the males sport a kangaroo-like pouch. During mating the male and female seahorse intertwine, the female depositing her eggs into the male's highly developed brood pouch. When the young are ready to hatch, the male seahorse goes through a series of jerky motions while holding fast to a plant stem or some other object with his tail. These movements open the pouch and the young colts emerge. The male pipefish displays a series of spiral corkscrew motions after the eggs are deposited into his pouch, apparently shaking down the eggs so that they are evenly distributed. The freshwater pipefish *Syngnathus spicifer* from Sri Lanka (Ceylon) has been bred in the aquarium, but the young are so small on hatching that nobody has succeeded as yet in raising them to maturity.

Taking the family for a swim

Most fishes, even those that protect their eggs, do not provide care for their young beyond the time of hatching. In fact, most of them will make a meal of any fry they can catch. There are some ex-

and herd them back into the group. As they move about, the parents can call their youngsters together by a typical movement, involving a shaking of the head and flapping of the pelvic fins. The young, in turn, recognize their parents, primarily by their typical movement and in some cases also by their color, as in the jewel fish *(Hemichromis bimaculatus)* and the firemouth *(Cichlasoma meeki)*. Young jewel fish followed orange-red disks, even if they had been reared from eggs in isolation and had never seen an adult fish in breeding colors. On the other hand, fire-

Closeup of brood pouch of "pregnant" male freshwater pipefish. Photo by A. Van den Nieuwenhuizen.

ceptions, of course. The bubble nest builders will attempt to ride herd on their young when they first become free swimming. They will catch any of their little wriggling offspring as they stray from under the bubble canopy and spit them back into the nest. But the most thorough care of their young is provided by the cichlids. While still in the "wriggler" stage, the young are tended by their parents and transferred frequently from one pit to another. Once they are free swimming, they are kept tightly bunched by their parents, who chase down stragglers

mouth youngsters reared without adults, followed all disks presented to them, without preference as to color, but those reared by their parents preferred models in which red occurred from about two weeks of age onward.

The factors inducing following responses of the young have been worked out in greatest detail in the mouthbreeding cichlids. In *Geophagus balzani*, for example, the young will return to the parent's mouth when danger threatens. Danger signals are the approach of large objects or turbulent currents. The parent, the

195

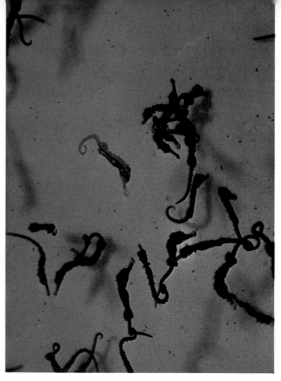

Closeup of brood pouch of male seahorse
(*Hippocampus*).

Newly hatched "colts."

Young emerging from male seahorse's brood pouch. Photos by William
M. Stephens.

The buccal cavity of this mottled morph of a female red top cichlid, *Labeotropheus trewavasae,* from Lake Malawi has taken on a peculiar distended appearance because she is carrying a mouthful of eggs. Photo by Hilmar Hansen, Aquarium Berlin.

The female *Geophagus balzani* has signaled for her young to return to the shelter of her mouth, and the young are rushing to comply. It seems impossible for them to fit in, but undoubtedly they will. Photo by Hans Joachim Richter.

Tilapia tholloni guarding young. This species is exceptional for a *Tilapia*, because it is a substrate breeder rather than a mouthbrooder.

Female *Tilapia mossambica* collecting her brood after taking the family for a swim. Photo by Gerhard Marcuse.

A pair of Nigerian mouthbrooders, *Haplochromis burtoni*, ready to spawn. Photo by Rudolf Zukal.

female in this case, opens her mouth and signals for the young to return to her. The young, as shown by experiments substituting models for the mother, swim toward dark patches, the underside of objects and recesses in solid surfaces. In case of the real parent, this combination is most likely to be the open mouth. They push inside and immediately fold their fins and allow themselves to sink motionless. In this way an almost incredible number of youngsters can crowd into the parent's mouth, even when grown quite a bit, although it is not unusual to see a number of tails protruding from the mother's mouth. Parents can distinguish their flock from strange youngsters, but will even herd *Daphnia* when their own young are not available.

A crowd of youngsters being taken for a "walk" by their parents is a sight that warms the cichlid fancier's heart. Close observation shows that the young of many species frequently make contact with the body of their parents, while they move slowly, surrounded by a cloud of baby fish. This behavior has been observed, for example, in *Tilapia mariae*, *Cichlasoma spilurum*, and *Cichlasoma labiatum*, the red devil. It has been shown to be essential for survival in the orange chromide (*Etroplus maculatus*) and the discus (*Symphysodon*). The orange chromide young make contact either with their mouth, nipping at the parent's side, or with a glancing sideswipe. Nipping at the parent's side is especially prevalent during the early phase of the youngster's free swim-

Aequidens curviceps guarding a depression in the bottom gravel into which it has transferred its brood. Photo by Hans Joachim Richter.

The firemouth cichlid youngsters, *Cichlasoma meeki*, recognize their parents by their bellies. Photo by Rudolf Zukal.

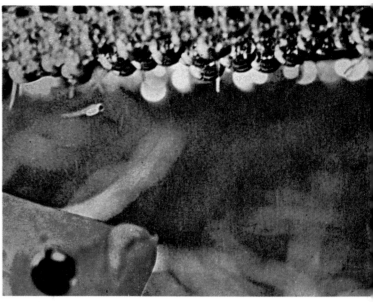

Male Siamese fighting fish tending his young in the bubble nest.

Oscars, *Astronotus ocellatus*, surrounded by a cloud of their offspring. Photo by H.J. Richter.

ming stage and can be shown to be a feeding response in which mucus secreted by special glands is ingested by the fry. The glancing consists of rubbing of the body of the young against that of their parents and seems to serve to keep youngsters and parents in a tight group. It reaches its maximum at a much later stage of development. Feeding on the mucus secretions of their parents was first discovered in discus fry *(Symphysodon discus* and *S. aequifasciata)*, where nutritive elements provided by the mucus appear to play an essential role in the diet of the young.

This photo by Gerhard Budich distinctly shows discus (*Symphysodon*) fry nibbling the surface of the skin of the parent. At this stage the fry are sufficiently large to be able to eat other types of food as well.

Chapter XII

SOCIAL LIFE

Species recognition

One of the great unsolved questions in the study of the behavior of fishes, and in fact all animals, pertains to the manner in which members of a species recognize each other. In fishes that raise their young to the free swimming stage it is conceivable that the babies learn to recognize their parents at an early age. That seems to be the case in mammals and most birds, with the exception of the parasitic breeders, such as the cuckoo and the cowbird. The study of cichlids under conditions where eggs or young were exchanged between two species showed development of preferences for the foster parents. There appeared to be an optimal period for this learning to occur. Later experience with their own species may, however, cause this preference to wane.

In conspicuously patterned fishes, it is a good guess to assume that the complex design serves a function of species recognition, as well as communication. Other means of recognition may be fin movements, patterns of swimming, sound production and chemical substances. The purpose of all these displays is to let other members of the same species know the presence of a potential mate or rival and to coordinate group actions. The function of the sense organs and perceptual organization may be keyed to these displays, so that the fish is able to suppress all irrelevant information from the environ-

ment and filter out all but the important influences of its surroundings. All this filtering of information may be compared to a person paying special attention to a particular individual in a crowd and ignoring all others to the point where it becomes impossible to recall later on who else was present in the group.

In a community tank it is easily observed how members of a particular species will pay attention to conspecifics, while more or less ignoring other fishes. The action may be courtship, territorial defense or schooling; only after the priority needs have been taken care of do these fishes interact with the other inhabitants of the tank, and even then they will show more interest in related species than in totally strange fishes. A similar picture emerges in natural communities. The reef dwellers form a community of many closely related, as well as unrelated fishes. Data gathered on the three-spot damselfish, *Eupomacentrus planifrons*, showed that each fish defended a territory. The defense perimeter, at which a stranger would be attacked, varied with the type of intruder. Conspecifics were attacked farthest away, other damselfish could approach closer, while unrelated fishes were allowed to come closest to the residence of a given fish. A different boundary line apparently applied in each case. Over a broad range, size within a given species played no role in this defense.

Jack Dempsey, *Cichlasoma octofasciatum*, guarding eggs. Photo by Rudolf Zukal.

The chanchito, *Cichlasoma facetum*, was the first cichlid bred in captivity. Photo by Gerhard Marcuse.

Orange chromide, *Etroplus maculatus*, and young. Photo by Rudolf Zukal.

Communication

Social behavior is based on the interaction of individuals and thus communication plays a key role. Visual signals are the equivalent of human gestures and body language. In fishes they start with the interaction of parents and young in species that take care of their offspring. The "follow-me" signal of the cichlid parent is an exaggeration of the normal intention

Tilapia tholloni tending eggs.

movement to swim away. Other signals are derived from spreading and collapsing of the dorsal fin, originally a call to the young to come to the nest, and eventually a warning of danger.

Color patterns play an important part in communication. The specific pattern displayed may signal threat or submission, depending on the particular circumstances. Usually an increase in area means threat, a folding of fins submission. Intense coloration also generally signals readiness to attack, a fading of colors precedes retreat. *Haplochromis wingati* displays vertical stripes in an aggressive mood, horizontal stripes when trying to escape.

A special case is the communication between species. The interaction of cleaner fish and their host represents a good example. The labroid wrasse *Labroides dimidiatus* signals its readiness to go to work by a special nodding of the head, followed by butting against the fins, gill covers and mouth of the fish it intends to clean. The host fish may actually have sought out the cleaner by moving to certain stations where cleaner fishes congregate. It invites the cleaner by opening its mouth and spreading its gill covers. While being picked over for parasites and bits of loose skin, the host fish holds perfectly still. The cleaner is rarely in danger of being swallowed. When the fish that is being cleaned is ready to move on, it signals its intention by partially closing its mouth with a jerky motion to tell the cleaners inside the mouth to leave and by shaking its body to signal the fishes on the outside to finish their job. Cleaner fish wear a special pattern of horizontal stripes to advertise themselves. It is this pattern that is imitated by the predatory mimics which take advantage of the cleaner's immunity from attack.

Many different species of fishes have the capability to act as cleaners. Some frequently observed cleaners, in addition to *Labroides*, are the cleaner goby *Gobio-*

soma oceanops, the butterfly fish *Chaetodon striatus*, and the damselfish *Abudefduf saxatilis*. Among customers of the cleaning services are not only bony fishes, but also manta rays, green turtles (cleaned by the damselfish *Abudefduf saxatilis* and the moon wrasse *Thalassoma lunare*) and crocodiles (picked over by a tooth carp, *Gambusia.*)

Communication by sound signals is probably more widespread than is presently apparent. Mating calls, territorial defense and warning cries have been identified. For example, sexually mature male *Tilapia mossambica* produce a low pitched drumming during their courtship. This sound appears to be associated with the visual signal movement of tail wagging. On days of spawning, sound production ceases about an hour before first oviposition and resumes upon completion of spawning. Visually isolated females exposed to the male drum sounds alone, laid their eggs several days earlier than females which were not exposed to this sound. Egg-carrying females gave off short drum sounds just prior to attacking approaching fish—apparently as a warning signal.

Olfaction also plays a role in signalling. Best known is probably the alarm substance released by skin injuries in Cypriniformes. At least one catfish, the common bullhead, *Ictalurus nebulosus*, and a goby, *Bathygobius soporator*, give off sex attractants.

Even less is known about the function of electrical signals. The South American gymnotid *Eigenmannia virescens* and the African gymnarchid *Gymnarchus niloticus* gave off a continuous discharge at a frequency of 250-500 Hz when fighting. Interruption of this electric signal for brief periods served as an aggressive threat. Subordinates changed the frequency of their discharge as they were being attacked. But *Eigenmannia* increased its frequency, while *Gymnarchus* decreased its frequency, in signalling their submission. The banded

Cichlasoma severum (albino variety) and young.
Photo by Kassanyi Jeno.

207

A pair of brown discus, *Symphysodon aequifasciata,* in front of their spawn (top). Closeup of the eggs (bottom). When discus fishes were first introduced, aquarium breeders had great difficulties in raising the young. By separating the young from their parents, they literally caused them to starve, until it was realized much later that discus fishes have evolved a mechanism to feed their fry by a thick, nutritious mucus secreted by special glands located on their parent's body. Photos by Dr. D. Terver, Nancy Aquarium.

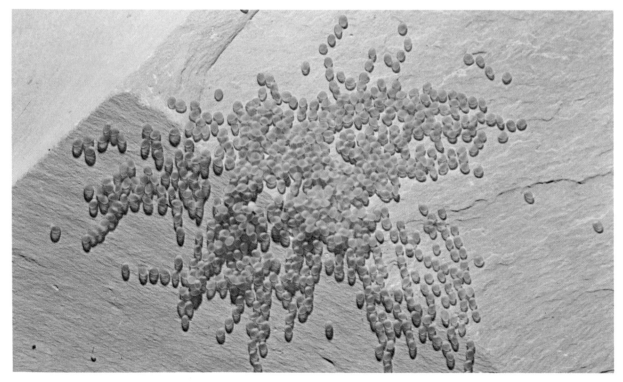

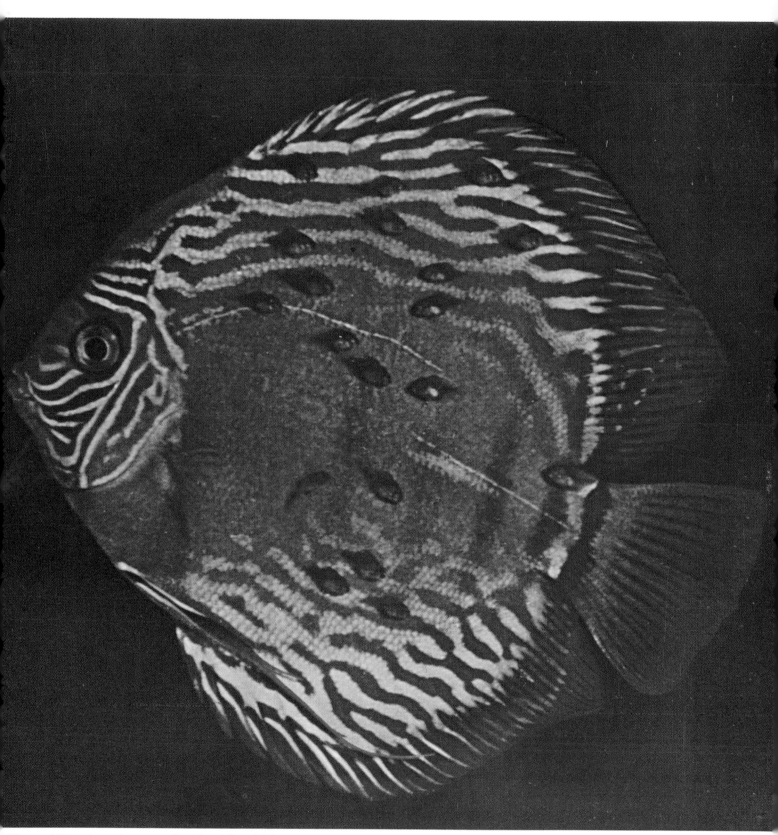

Discus (*Symphysodon aequifasciata*) fry picking nutrient mucus off their parent's side. Photo by Dr. Eduard Schmidt.

Tilapia mariae and young. The young differ so much from the adult in appearance that they were at first classified as an entirely different species, *Tilapia meeki*. Photo by Gerhard Marcuse.

Tilapia mossambica spawning. The female (front) is just picking up the eggs which she has deposited in a depression, after which the male (back) has fertilized them. Note the breeding tube of the male. Photo by Chvojka Milan.

Tilapia mariae taking two-week-old offspring for a "walk." Photo by Gerhard Marcuse.

knifefish *Gymnotus carapo* has four types of electric signals. Its unmodified discharge aids in recognizing conspecifics. Sharp increases in frequency, followed by decrease to the original level served as threat display. Discharge breaks of about one-and-a-half seconds also served as threat, but indicated a greater tendency to flee. Cessation of discharge for longer periods was associated with retreat and could be considered an appeasement signal. Recently it has been claimed that a wide variety of fish species also are capable of communicating by a kind of electromagnetic signal similar to, but not quite like the impulses we pick up on a radio receiver.

Color patterns of *Tilapia mariae* change considerably during maturation. (Top) Immature; (middle) juvenile; (bottom) adult. Top photo by Dr. Karl Knaack, middle and bottom photos by Dr. Herbert R. Axelrod.

The cleaner wrasse, *Labroides dimidiatus*, at work picking parasites off a large grouper (*Epinephelus*). Photo by Walter Deas.

Another, but lesser known cleaner, *Labrichthys quadrilineata*, is seen here cleaning a surgeon fish, *Acanthurus bleekeri*. Photo by Aaron Norman.

Blue-finned trevally, *Caranx melampygus*, are predaceous surface feeders. The young and immature school, whereas adults have a lesser tendency to aggregate. Photo by Rodney Jonklaas.

The green knifefish, *Eigenmannia virescens*, emits a continuous electrical signal when fighting. Photo by Gerhard Marcuse.

Schooling

Many fishes aggregate with other members of their own species or with relatives to form schools. Most important to fisheries are the huge schools of commercially important food fishes, such as the herring *(Clupea harengus)*, cod *(Gadus)*, mullet *(Mugil)* and tuna *(Thunnus)*. Schools of over a million individuals have been reported in these species. Among popular aquarium fishes there are many schooling species, including such favorites as the cardinal tetra *Cheirodon axelrodi* and the zebra fish *Brachydanio rerio*. As a general rule, barbs and characins school, while anabantids, cichlids and cyprinodonts don't. But even in solitary species the young will form schools that only break up when individuals become large enough to display their aggressive tendencies toward their nest mates.

Schooling appears to be mostly dependent on visual signals. Each fish in the aggregation takes his cue from his neighbor in keeping his position in the group. Visual contact is indicated by the fact that most fish schools disperse at night. On the other hand, there are observations that blind fish, such as the blind cave characin, are capable of schooling. Presumably lateral line or chemical cues serve to keep members of the school in touch with one another under these circumstances.

Pennant butterflyfishes, *Heniochus acuminatus*, are often seen in large groups feeding near coral reefs. New York Zoological Society.

Labroides dimidiatus cleaning an anemonefish (*Amphiprion melanopus*). Photo by Allan Power.

Their tendency to school is typical of characins, such as these gold tetras, *Hemigrammus armstrongi*. Photo by Dr. Herbert R. Axelrod.

Chapter XIII

MODIFICATION OF BEHAVIOR

Habituation

All organisms can change their reactions in the light of experience. Differences exist in the degree of modification that is possible, the complexity of the activity and the length of time such changes are retained. This ability is essential for the survival of the individual and the species. The process of learning parallels the changes that are found in evolution on a much longer time scale, as the famous psychologist B. F. Skinner and others have pointed out.

The simplest form of learning consists of cessation of reacting to some kind of repeated stimulation. This type of learning is known as *habituation*. It can be distinguished from *desensitization* by the fact that the introduction of a novel situation will bring the response back to normal. In the aquarium, habituation can be observed when a fish is newly introduced into a tank. The initial fright reaction disappears as the fish becomes habituated to its new surroundings. But transfer the fish to another aquarium tank and the whole sequence will start over again.

Conditioning

Many events in a fish's environment trigger responses that can be conditioned. The signal for this response must be paired with some event that normally would not evoke any response, or at least not this particular one. After a sufficient number of pairings, the previously neutral event becomes a signal for the animal to respond with the activity that originally could be evoked only by its appropriate kind of stimulation. One could, for example, turn the lights on and off a couple of times before dropping food into a tank. Normally the fishes would not respond with any particular behavior to the light. But by repeatedly pairing the light with food, the fishes will have become conditioned to the light and will rise to the surface in the expectation of being fed every time the light flashes on. The previously neutral event has now become a signal for food.

Scientific investigators often make use of electrical shock, rather than food, as a signal for conditioning. In one application, weak electrical shock to the side of a fish was paired with brief flashes of light. Originally shock alone elicited a movement of the fish's tail. Eventually tail movement became conditioned, so that it followed whenever the light alone was turned on. This method provides a very sensitive index of the fish's ability to see the light. A very precise method that can be used to measure perception of movement and many other kinds of reactions, utilizes conditioning of the rate that the heart beats. A goldfish is confined to a sponge-lined chamber, set within a 50 gallon aquarium. When the goldfish is mildly shocked, its heart rate decreases. This change can be picked up by an

Bar jacks, *Caranx ruber*, feeding on plankton attracted by an underwater light. Photo by Walter Starck II.

electrocardiograph to which the fish is connected. Black spots were projected to move in front of the fish and paired with shock. The fish was soon conditioned to slow its heart rate to the visual signal, giving scientists the opportunity to test exactly the rate at which a goldfish detects motion.

One of the essential needs for this kind of learning, known as *classical conditioning*, is that the fish must already have the response that is to be conditioned in its behavior pattern. The new signal becomes a substitute for the normal environmental event that usually calls for this behavior. Subtle differences remain in the animal's response to the new signal, but these will only be noticed in a detailed analysis of time relationships and other slight changes. No systematic differences between species are apparent. With appropriate controls, it appears that the number of times a light

and shock must be paired before the appearance of conditioned responses to the onset of light is about the same in fish, pigs and rhesus monkeys, with monkeys requiring a few more trials than either pigs or fish.

Learning and problem solving

The examples of learning given so far do not account for the appearance of new response patterns. If we put a paddle into a small aquarium housing a hungry *Tilapia* and drop a *Tubifex* worm into the tank every time the fish hits the paddle, we will soon find our fish working as fast as it can eat. Since the fish never encountered paddles that dispense worms in its previous life, we can be sure that it has learned a new response. For another example, we might put a fish into a tank that is divided by a small barrier into two compartments. Pipe a sound of an auditory

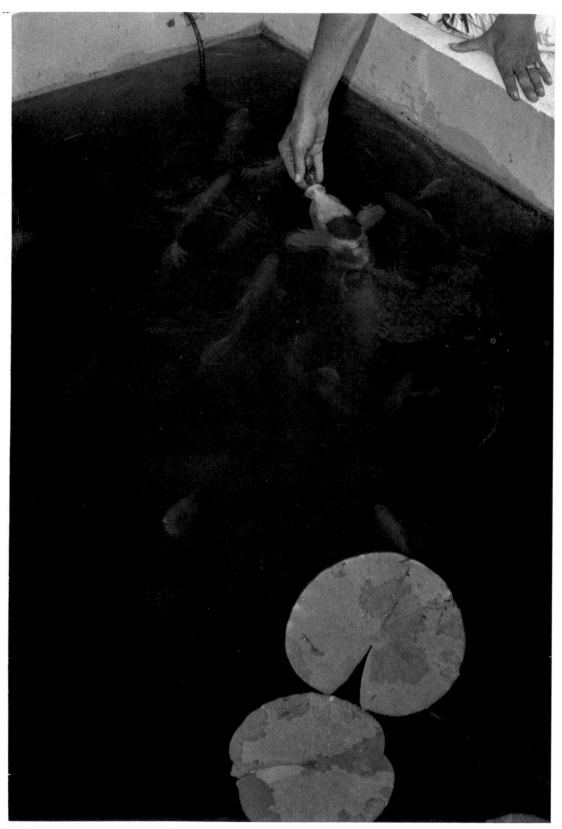

Koi (*Cyprinus carpio*) are easily trained to accept food from their owner's hand. Photo by Dr. Herbert R. Axelrod.

Cardinal tetras, *Cheirodon axelrodi*, quickly adapt to feeding on freeze-dried *Tubifex*. Photo by Dr. Herbert R. Axelrod.

Tubifex worms are a preferred food for many fishes. These reddish worms live in individual tubes in the mud of slow-moving polluted streams. When held in containers, they aggregate into a ball of tightly intertwined individuals. Photo by Dr. Herbert R. Axelrod.

frequency that the fish can hear into the tank, followed by a weak electric shock. As might be expected, the fish will try to escape the shock, and after a while will swim across the barrier into the other compartment. The moment of crossing the barrier interrupts a light beam falling on a photocell and triggers the switch that turns off the shock. Repeated trials will teach the fish to escape into the other compartment very quickly. Ultimately the fish can avoid shock completely by reacting in time to the onset of sound as a warning signal. *Our fish is getting an education!*

Both kinds of learning are illustrative of two closely related kinds of conditioning, *operant* conditioning and *instrumental* conditioning. They share the property that the consequences of an activity increase or decrease the tendency to repeat the response at the next opportunity. In operant conditioning, the fish hitting the paddle, the subject itself determines the rate of re-

sponding; in instrumental conditioning, the escape or avoidance reaction, an external factor determines the spacing of trials.

The contingencies of rewarding or punishing experiences that follow a given act are the key to this kind of learning. *Positive reinforcement*, food in this case, and the cessation of *negative reinforcement*, shock termination in the example, strengthen the previous response; negative reinforcement and the withdrawal of prior positive reinforcement suppress or weaken a previous response. These contingencies are always present in the life of fishes. For every possible response there are many alternatives. The consequences of each action determines which of the alternatives the fish will choose.

These general principles hold for a wide range of animals. As one might expect, however, there are differences too. Rats and some fishes differ, for example, in the

Shown above is a veiltail goldfish with normal eyes. The celestial goldfish (below) is a special breed of goldfish from the Far East whose eyes are directed upward. It is not possible for the fish to see anything from the sides and beneath. It is definitely incapable of competing with any fish with normal vision. Top photo by Rudolf Zukal, bottom photo by G. Marcuse.

Groupers such as this coral grouper, *Cephalopholis miniatus*, often become friendly to divers, unless they have been persecuted by spear fishing. Note the cleaner fish at work on the grouper's side. Photo by Allan Power.

An African dwarf cichlid (*Pelvicachromis taeniatus*) observing the observer. Photo by Hans Joachim Richter.

(Top) An artificial tide-pool was used to study the jumping behavior of the goby, *Bathygobius soporator* (see p. 227). Shown here at "low tide," this pool could be flooded at "high tide" so that the large compartment in the foreground and the three small pools in the background were under water. During experiments, gobies were permitted to explore pools overnight, then placed in one of the two small pools farthest from the camera, after the water level was lowered. Well-oriented gobies jumped into the middle pool, then into large compartment (left). Photos by Dr. Lester R. Aronson. (Reproduced with permission from Annals New York Academy of Sciences, 1971, vol. 188).

reversal learning task. Given the choice between two colored disks, *Tilapia* and goldfish have been trained to pick one color in preference to the other by reinforcing one target with *Tubifex*. After achieving this discrimination, the colors are switched, so that the previously positive choice is now no longer rewarded, but hitting the alternate target will now pay off in worms. The fishes learn to reverse their choice, but apparently do not profit from their experience. At least they fail to improve their performance by learning faster in further reversals. Rats, faced with the same task will take longer on the first reversal, but improve steadily with practice from then on. These findings do not seem to have complete generality, however. Recent experiments on *Astronotus ocellatus* showed very good discrimination reversal learning, using a slightly different set of targets, a white cross on a green background versus a white triangle on a red background.

Under natural conditions, fishes are capable of learning quite complex relationships. The tide-pool dwelling goby *Bathygobius soporator*, for example, can be observed to jump from one rock pool to another when the tide is out, although it cannot possibly see the location of the target pool at the time of jumping. It has been shown that these fishes survey the location of pools during high tide and retain this knowledge for use when needed during low tide. Memory persists for at least a month, as tests have shown. One overnight stay in an artificial pool at "high tide" is sufficient for this learning to occur.

The jewel fish, *Hemichromis bimaculatus*, in recent studies, has been observed to make directed jumps out of small pools in sand depressions or out of small enclosed spaces with opaque sides. Memory of previous locations was one of the factors that determined the direction the fish took. Aquarium fanciers who wonder how their prize specimens manage to jump out of their tank through almost incredibly small openings might take notice.

Jewel fish, *Hemichromis bimaculatus*, have been observed to make directed jumps out of small depressions in the sand. Memory of previous locations was one of the factors that determined direction of jump. Photo by Kassanyi Jeno.

Tilapia mossambica, a good subject for learning experiments. Males produce a low-pitched "drum" sound during courtship. Photo by Hilmar Hansen, Aquarium Berlin.

Ribbon eels, *Rhinomuraena ambonensis*, often take advantage of the smallest openings in an aquarium cover to make their escape. Photo by Kok-Hang Choo, Taipei Aquarium.

Koi, an ornamental carp, originating in Japan, become very tame.

Oscars, *Astronotus ocellatus,* seem to recognize their owners very readily. Photo by Dr. Herbert R. Axelrod.

Consideration of the complexity of learning brings us to some questions that are invariably asked of comparative psychologists: Where do fishes stand in intelligence, compared to a dog, for example, and are some fishes more intelligent than others? It used to be thought that one could arrange all the different animals on a rough scale of intelligence, ranging from fish to man and correlating nicely with brain development. Attempts were made to invent simple instruments, such as mazes and problem tasks, that could be used at many different levels and would result eventually in a neat arrangement of species in some ascending order. These attempts were doomed to failure. The task is not that simple. As it happens, each species has become adapted, as best as it can, to the particular problems it has faced in evolution. Instead of a single ability to learn, that could be called intelligence, there are many abilities. Among the factors that determine how well an animal performs are *response availability*, fishes have a limited capacity for manipulation, compared to a monkey; *sensory dominance*, visual cues are more important to a cichlid than to a rat; and *preparedness*, the tendency to quickly learn behavior patterns that have survival value for the species concerned, compared to tasks that are irrelevant.

These considerations also hold true for comparisons of intelligence between different species of fish. Take one example, a comparison of goldfish *(Carassius auratus)* and Siamese fighting fish *(Betta splendens)* in a learning task employing the avoidance conditioning procedure. As mentioned before, the fish avoids shock by swimming from one compartment of the apparatus into another at the onset of a sound cue. Goldfish learned considerably more rapidly to avoid the shock than bettas, and, indeed, more rapidly than most mammals trained in the same task. This difference reflected species differences in adaptation and characteristic responses to shock, not differences in learning ability. Goldfish are bottom

feeders and flight is their typical reaction to the abrupt onset of intense stimulation. *Bettas,* on the other hand, are aggressive predators. Their most likely response to shock is immobility or aggression. Flight responses are much more likely to acquaint the fish with the escape opportunity and thus result in faster learning than immobility or attack, which do not give the fish the chance to be reinforced.

Notwithstanding these purely rational arguments, the devoted fish watcher will discover differences in the apparent intelligence of his fishes. These are not related so much to the ability of the fish to solve its particular problem as they are to the way humans are accustomed to think. Large cichlids, particularly, such as the oscar *(Astronotus ocellatus)*, give the appearance of superior intelligence. They are visual and one can tell from their eyes where they are looking. They are aggressive and not easily frightened. While most fishes in an aquarium will soon learn to distinguish between their owner and his family, and strangers, large cichlids become particularly tame, take tidbits from their owner's fingers and rise to the surface to beg for food. They will even allow themselves to be touched. In addition they are usually very good parents. All these traits combine to make large cichlids appear to be the most intelligent of common aquarium fishes.

How to train a fish

A few basic principles suffice to permit anyone to teach a fish to perform some simple tasks. Let us take training a fish to swim through a ring as our example. Start with one large ring and a hungry fish. Actually, most of the cichlids of my acquaintance will not have to be especially starved, as they always seem to be hungry. At first the fish will probably avoid swimming through the ring, but don't worry, eventually it will do so. Do not try to force the fish, because that would be aversive. Drop food into the tank, even if the fish swims only close by the ring. Gradually the fish will learn to stay near the ring. As the fish improves, cut down on rewarding near misses and only reinforce the behavior you want. This whole process of gradual approximation is called *shaping* and it is a key element in any training procedure.

Once the fish has learned to swim through the ring consistently, one can move in several directions. One could introduce smaller and smaller rings. Fishes that could never be trained to swim through a small ring directly will learn to do so if taken through a number of steps. Different kinds of tasks could be added, such as a series of rings or a paddle that has to be hit, forming a behavior chain. A signal can be introduced, so that the fish will perform on command. Simply reinforce only when the signal is present and do not reward when the signal is absent.

A number of precautions should be observed. Always remove the ring, paddle or other device when not in use, as the fish will quickly stop doing his act if he is not reinforced for it. Fishes can only be trained to perform tasks which they are equipped to do. Surface loving fishes perform best at the surface, bottom dwellers at the bottom. You can get a *Betta* to assume his fighting posture on command or a mormyrid to put out an electrical pulse, but obviously you cannot do the reverse.

Once a behavior pattern has been established, it is all right to reward only every so often, rather than every time the fish performs correctly. This so-called *partial reinforcement* leads to a tendency to perform the act for a longer time, even if no more reinforcement is given. There is an interesting difference between fish and white laboratory rats with respect to this effect. If a 50 per cent and a 100 per cent reinforcement group of rats are compared with each other, the performance of the 50 per cent group always outlasts that of the 100 per cent group after feeding is discontinued, regardless of whether the number of trials or the number of reinforcements are equated. (You can't equate both.) In fish, however, the effect can only be demonstrated if the number of reinforcements is equated (and there are therefore twice the number of trials), but not when the total of trials is the same for both groups.

Shown here is the well known electric eel *Electrophorus electricus* of the Amazon. Photographed in a tank by Klaus Paysan.

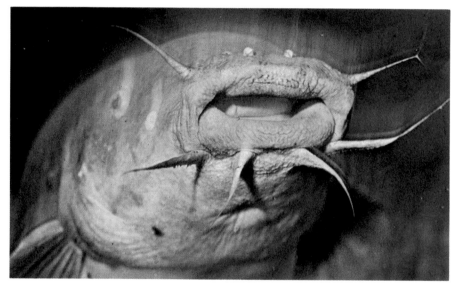

Closeup of the mouth region of the electric catfish *Malapterurus electricus*. Photo by Klaus Paysan.

Viewed externally it is not possible to recognize the location of the electric organs of the electric catfish *Malapterurus electricus*. These organs are embedded in the fatty tissues beneath the skin. Photo by Dr. Eugene Balon.

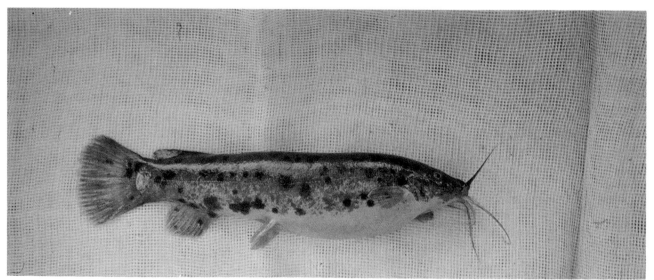

Astroscopus is a genus of stargazers (Uranoscopidae) with electric organs. Shown here is a non-electric stargazer, *Ichthyoscopus lebeck*. Photo by Dr. Shih-chieh Shen.

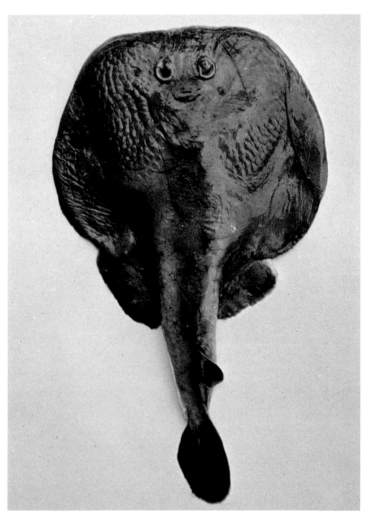

The electric organs of this electric ray, *Narke japonicus*, are easily recognized. They are situated between the eyes and pectoral fins. Photo by Dr. Shih-chieh Shen.

Chapter XIV

ELECTRIC ORGANS, ELECTRORECEPTION AND ELECTROLOCATION

A shocking story

If people were able to identify things by radar, communicate by radio and send out electric shocks to defend themselves, all without benefit of complicated technical equipment, this chapter would be up in front of this book, together with the discussion of the other senses. But, as of now, no such abilities have been found in mankind, so they seem strange and wonderful to us and deserve special treatment.

There are two types of electric fish. The strongly electric fishes include the electric eel *(Electrophorus)*, the electric catfish *(Malapterurus)*, electric rays (Torpedinidae), and the stargazer *(Astroscopus)*. They can generate an electric shock strong enough to stun their prey or to discourage a predator. The weakly electric fishes include the African mormyrids (Mormyridae), the South American knife fishes (Gymnotoidei), the African knife fish *Gymnarchus* and some marine rays and skates *(Raja)*. All except the last group use their electric organs in electrolocation, the detection of the distortions of an electric field by objects in the environment. They probably also signal to one another electrically by alterations of their discharge frequencies. Electroreceptors alone have also been demonstrated in some catfish, the brown bullhead, *Ictalurus nebulosus*, and the glass catfish, *Kryptopterus bicirrhis*, for example, and most, if not all, sharks (Elasmobranchi).

Strongly electric fish have been known since antiquity. Electric rays *(Torpedo)* are said to have been used by the Romans for a kind of nonconvulsive electric shock therapy. The nature of weakly electric fishes was not recognized until the 1950's, although some structures were identified earlier as "pseudoelectrical" on anatomical grounds. It is possible that the ancient Egyptians may have been familiar with the electrical properties of weakly electrical fishes of the Nile, as their discharge, while weak, is perceptible to the touch.

The electrical generating cells of all species consists of modified muscle tissue, except for the South American knife fish family Sternarchidae (for example, the black ghost, *Sternarchus albifrons)*, where the organ is of neural origin. Ordinary nerve and muscle cells generate electric potentials in their normal functioning. Electric organs generate increased potentials by the arrangement of the cells, their synchronous activity and by special structures that channel the flow of electric current. Strong electric discharges are intermittent; weakly electrical organs emit constant pulses continually.

The electric eel *(Electrophorus electricus)*, a member of the gymnotid group from South America, has the highest output of electrical potential, more than 500 volts. It also has a smaller pulse of about 10 volts that it uses for electrolocation and communication. Its large output is used to stun prey and as a defense. The electric catfish, *Malapterurus electricus*, can reach over 300 volts potential in its discharge. The remaining two types of strongly electric fishes inhabit a marine environment. The electric rays are a large cosmopolitan group. They are sluggish and use their discharge to catch faster moving fishes. Their discharge was measured as high as 220 volts in *Torpedo nobilana*.

In some electric rays, for example in *Narcine brasiliensis*, a second accessory weak electric organ serves electrolocation and electric signalling functions. The stargazers, *Astroscopus*, occur in the North and South Atlantic. They lie in wait, covered by sand up to their eyes, for unwary small food fishes. Their discharge is measured at about 50 volts. The only other marine fishes known to be capable of electric discharges are the rays and skates of the genus *Raja*. Their output consists of weak, long-lasting single pulses, which they emit infrequently when violently stimulated. The purpose of these discharges is presently unknown.

The discharge of the electric catfish, *Malapterurus electricus*, can reach a potential of over 300 volts. Photo by Klaus Paysan.

The black ghost, *Sternarchus albifrons*, is one of the weakly electric fishes. This family differs from all the other weakly electric fishes because the electric generating system is of neural origin. Photo by Harald Schultz.

The banded knifefish, *Gymnotus carapo,* a weakly electric fish from South America.

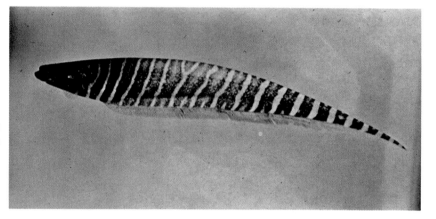

Gnathonemus tamandua, one of the African mormyrids. Photo by Dr. Herbert R. Axelrod.

The glass catfish, *Kryptopterus bicirrhis*, has electroreceptors distributed all over its body. Photo by Hilmar Hansen, Aquarium Berlin.

The African knife fish *Gymnarchus niloticus*. Photo by Klaus Paysan.

Fish radar

The output of the electric organs of the weakly electric freshwater fishes, the mormyrids, the gymnotids and *Gymnarchus*, as well as a secondary output of some of the strongly electric fishes, consists of continuous pulses. These fishes also have an electric receptor system consisting of a modified lateral line organ. The receptors may be used passively to detect electrical signals; they are also used actively as a radar-like electrolocating system.

The various types of receptor organs are widely distributed over the body. There are two kinds, *tonic receptors* giving long-lasting responses to low frequency stimulation, and *phasic receptors* which are sensitive to high frequency impulses to which they respond with brief bursts of activity. The receptors are extremely sensitive. They pick up minute voltage gradients, interpreting them in terms of differences of conductivity of surrounding objects. Metal objects, for example, are easily differentiated from non-conductors.

The fishes can be trained to make use of their abilities under laboratory conditions. Blinded mormyrids, *(Gnathonemus petersi)* for example, learned to distinguish between metal and plastic rods when one had food attached to it and the other did not. The majority of subjects avoided the metal rod initially, but could be trained to prefer it to the plastic rod when it was paired with food. Attacks on metal objects are commonly observed in aggressive species, such as *Gymnotus* and *Electrophorus*. Even more amazing was their ability to distinguish a horizontal from a vertical electric field.

All weakly electric fishes hold their body relatively rigid when swimming. It is thought that this posture stabilizes the electric field. The knife fishes (Gymnotidae) and *Gymnarchus* have the strange habit of swimming backward and forward with equal facility. An interesting explanation has been advanced. The physical configuration of their electrical field has its maximum just outside the tail. It is likely then that the backward approach in exploration of new situations is based on the superior electrolocating characteristics of this seemingly strange behavior. It is also interesting, in this connection, that knife fishes attack each other on the tail when fighting. If damaged, the tail has the power to regenerate. Gymnotids have been caught in the wild with partially regenerated tails.

Electric signals

Under natural conditions the main function of the electric organs is the detection of prey and other features of the environment. It is also possible that fishes may use their electric capacity in orientation by detection of currents induced by the earth's magnetic field. A third, recently discovered function is the capability of communication with other species members by electrical signals.

The basis of communication is the ability of these fishes to control the pulse frequency and sequence of signal output. Signal acceleration occurs naturally as response to changes in the environment and the presence of electrical pulses, such as might be produced by another weakly electrical fish. It can be classically conditioned. Signal frequency has also been brought under the control of operant conditioning in laboratory experiments. If the animal is presented with electrical pulses of a frequency that matches the frequency of its own output, it will sometimes shift its own frequency away from the interfering alien frequency. An experimenter can "chase" the fish's frequency up and down within a certain range; beyond this range the fish will fairly rapidly change its own frequency to the other side of the interfering signal. Another response to electric pulses at the fish's own frequency may be a complete cessation of discharge. This reaction is thought to be related to aggressive behavior of other electric fishes. It may represent a kind of submissive behavior or perhaps the fish is "hiding."

A thorough study has been made of the social role of electric discharges of the banded knifefish *Gymnotus carapo*.* Up to six individuals were observed in a large aquarium that contained many hiding places for these nocturnal and secretive fishes. The dominant fishes established defended territories, while the subordinates succeeded only in holding on to a single hiding place temporarily. Electrical discharge frequencies were monitored continuously. The fishes were resting by day; swimming activity commenced when the lights went out. They had a characteristic electrical discharge pattern that ranged from 36.5 Hz (pulses/second) to 56 Hz at rest and from 56 Hz to 67 Hz when active. Sharp temporary increases in discharge frequency occurred during fighting or when pursuing goldfish that were used for food. The subordinate fish completely suspended his discharge in response to the aggressive displays of an opponent. Attacks on other *Gymnotus* were more frequent than attacks on other weakly electric fishes and much more frequent than on non-electric fishes. These differences were based on electrical recognition of conspecifics which were identified and located by their discharge patterns.*

* Further details may be found in: Patricia Black-Cleworth, The role of electrical discharges in the non-reproductive social behavior of *Gymnotus carapo* (Gymnotidae, Pisces) in *Animal Behaviour Monographs*, 1970, vol. 3, part 1.

* It should be noted that all signals discussed so far are based on pulsed electric currents and act over a relatively short distance. The recently claimed discovery of radio-like signals in a wide variety of fishes needs further confirmation.

The mormyrid *Gnathonemus petersi* uses its long snout for locating food buried in the sand or mud. New York Zoological Society photo.

Green sunfish, *Lepomis cyanellus* (top) and a pike cichlid, *Crenicichla saxatilis* (bottom) have been shown to utilize sun's position for direction finding (see p. 246). Photo above by Aaron Norman; lower photo by Gerhard Marcuse.

The black acara, *Aequidens portalegrensis*, shown here spawning (top) and guarding eggs (bottom), was a subject in sun orientation experiments. Photos by Rudolf Zukal.

Chapter XV

HOW FISHES FIND THEIR WAY

Orientation

It is unlikely that the guppy will ever replace the racing pigeon, but the capability of fishes for long-distance orientation does indeed match that of birds. Pin-point accuracy in navigation, journeys of thousands of miles through the trackless ocean and efficient homing have all been observed in fishes. Although there is no evidence that there is any direct ancestral relationship, the same problems have arisen many times during evolution and have been solved in analogous ways.*

Orientation refers to a process by which an animal establishes its position with respect to a point in space and time. There always exists a reference source to which the direction of the animal's movement can be related. If this reference source is the animal's own body, the resulting behavior is a search. A single external reference, a compass would be a well-known example, establishes a movement direction. Two independent reference points are necessary to define a position uniquely, like a grid on a map. Many different reference sources may be used, singly or in combination. While the problem of orientation remains the same, there are many solutions.

Anything but a random movement is based on some kind of orientation, and it is a good guess that fishes do not engage in truly random movement. That does not mean that a fish is always swimming toward some long-distance goal. Most orientation takes place to local environmental features such as shorelines, rocks, caves and plants, as well as gradients of temperature, salinity, smells and sounds. Fishes newly introduced into an aquarium explore actively and soon familiarize themselves with the tank's dimensions and major features, hiding places, sources of food and their companions, if any.

Biorhythms

If you feed your fishes every day at the same time, you will soon see them congregate at the surface a little before the daily feeding time. They will also react much more strongly to you entering the room at that time, than they normally do. They have been conditioned to expect food at a particular time. They can tell when the feeding is due by their sense of time, often called their internal clock. Fishes share this ability to tell time with plants, other animals and man. Its origin is not yet known, but its usefulness is undisputed. The basis of time orientation is a biological rhythm of about 24 hours. This rhythm is only apparent under artificial conditions of constant darkness or constant light, as normal changes of day and night, constant daily feeding time or any other important

* For a fuller discussion, the interested reader may consult: H. E. Adler, Ontogeny and phylogeny of orientation. *In* Development and evolution of behavior, edited by L. R. Aronson, E. Tobach, D. S. Lehrman and J. S. Rosenblatt. W. H. Freeman, San Francisco, California, 1970, pages 303–336.

events in the life of fishes with a daily regularity synchronizes the biological rhythm with the periodic influences in the environment.

In fact, there are probably a number of independent biorhythms of about 24 hours duration running concurrently. They can be teased apart experimentally, but are coordinated by the normal change of light and dark or other periodic events in a fish's life. Pre-feeding activity periods are the most obvious. They have been studied not only in fish, but also in bees, birds and rats. We can compare this rhythm with human hunger pangs. People get used to eating at at certain time and will begin to feel hungry just when the accustomed meal time comes around. If you travel across a few time zones by jet, this internal clock makes you feel hungry at odd times, like 3 o'clock in the morning, but you can't eat a thing at the regular time when local meals are served. We call it jet lag and it affects not only eating, but many other body functions as well. After a week or so, the internal clock adjusts to local time. The same story holds true for fishes. When a definite feeding routine is established in an aquarium, the fishes are often startled when fed at an unaccustomed time and may even refuse to eat at first. On the other hand, fish fed at random are seldom disturbed by the appearance of food and will go to work right away to clean up the goodies.

There are many other rhythmic behavior patterns. Swimming activity follows a definite cycle. Some fishes are day active, others are active at night, to cite one example. Obviously this is a 24 hour rhythm, controlled by the onset of light or darkness. Some species show a predawn peak of swimming. Bluegill sunfish *(Lepomis macrochirus)* and largemouth bass *(Micropterus salmoides)*, for example, were confined in tanks that automatically recorded their activity. A peak of swimming activity was found to precede the onset of light by about one to three hours. Shifting the artificial day-night cycle caused a shift in activity that was completed in from ten to twenty days. The shift back to the original pattern was much faster. It took only two to three days for the old peak to reappear.

The light shock reaction is another periodic response that shows a biorhythm. Light shock is easily observed when a tank is suddenly illuminated after the lights had been turned off at the usual "bed" time. The fishes react to the bright light by losing their color, slowly sinking to the bottom of the tank, where they stay immobile for a while, fan their fins without moving or swim back and forth slowly, sometimes bumping into obstacles. After a while they recover from their shock and start to go about their normal business. The time it takes them to recover changes during the period they are in the dark. It is zero right after the lights are turned out, rises gradually to a maximum of more than five minutes after some four hours in the dark and then decreases gradually until it reaches a minimum of about a minute just before the lights would normally have been turned on again. Light shock can be totally avoided, incidentally, by building a gradual dawning into the lighting system of an aquarium.

Tidal rhythms may be superimposed on the daily activity cycle. The small blenny *Coryphoblennius galerita* lives in rock pools and feeds mainly on barnacles. Its activity shows a strong rhythm with a periodicity of 12.5 hours, just about the period of the tidal cycle. This rhythm persists in the laboratory for at least five days and can also be recorded in complete darkness.

Biorhythms may play an important role in navigation. We shall see later in this chapter that one of the references that fishes may use in orientation is the position of the sun. The sun is a good cue to position, but only if the time is known. In the northern hemisphere it rises in the east and pursues an apparent path that reaches its highest point at local noon, when it points south, only to descend until it sets

Spanish mackerel, *Scomberomorus maculatus*, like most other mackerels, move northward as the water gets warmer.

European perch, *Perca fluviatilis*, travel to the shallow parts of the stream, pond, or lake to spawn. Photo by D. Terver, Nancy Aquarium.

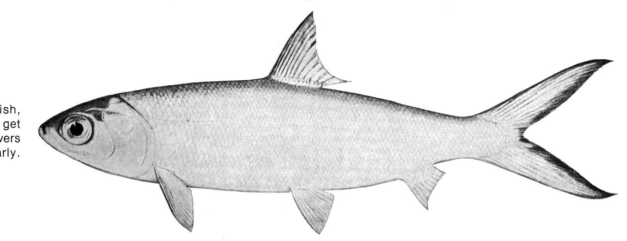

Asiatic milkfish, *Chanos chanos*, get in and out of rivers irregularly.

Large schools of the snub-dart, *Trachinotus blochii*, visit the coast of Queensland, Australia, in the winter months. Photo by Allan Power.

in the west. As long as the fish can compensate for the sun's movement, it can keep a constant course by swimming at an angle to the sun's apparent position, although this angle changes constantly during the course of a day. It is essential, however, for the fish to have an accurate time sense to accomplish this feat.

Experiments have confirmed the capacity of some fishes to make these judgments. A specially designed circular tank was used. It had a small starting compartment in its center in which a fish was placed. Around the tank were 16 small compartments in which the fish could find refuge. Only one compartment was open during the initial learning phase of any one experiment. This opening always lay in the same compass direction. After the fish had become acquainted with the location of the safe compartment, it was tested with all 16 boxes open. The experimenter recorded which of the compartments the fish would enter. A majority of choices of the right compartment in the absence of other cues indicated that the fish used sun orientation.

Green sunfish *(Lepomis cyanellus)* and the black acara *(Aequidens portalegrensis)* were subjects in the original experiment. Mirrors could be used to change the apparent direction of the sun, with the result that the fishes would reorient accordingly. The apparent day-night cycle was shifted by keeping fishes in an artificial change of light and dark. When they had become accustomed to this new cycle, four days later, they interpreted the sun's position in terms of this new time schedule.

The pike cichlid, *Crenicichla saxatalis,* seemed to be especially well suited for these experiments, in another series of tests. Two trials were sometimes sufficient to teach these pike-like predators the location of their potential hiding place. An artificial sun, actually a 300 watt light bulb, could also be used as a substitute for the real thing, as the fishes accepted it as a reference source, but in most cases they merely oriented to it at a fixed angle, rather than compensating for movement, as they would have done for the real sun.

Fishes proved capable of reacting to the height of the sun at a given time, as well as to its relative movement around the horizon. At the equator, where the sun switches between reaching its highest point at noon in a northerly direction from March to September and in the south from September to March, fishes compensated for these annual changes, as well as reacting to the daily course of the sun's motion. It appears then that fishes can orient to the movement of the sun by taking into account the changes from light to dark and the length of the day, as well as the annual cycle of the height of the sun.

The annual cycle must also play a rôle in initiating long distance journeys of the many species of fish that undertake regular migrations. It is by no means clear on what basis these seasonal movements occur, but it is quite likely that the regular changes in the sun's height and the associated changes in the length of the day and water temperature play an important role.

The lunar cycle affects the ocean's tides, so it should not be surprising that it also is a major influence on the life cycle of some fishes. One of the most spectacular events that depend directly on the moon's phases is the spawning of the grunion *(Leuresthes tenius)* along certain beaches in southern California. Due to the moon's gravitational pull on the ocean, the highest tides occur at the full moon and the new moon. Grunion appear on the beaches to spawn at these high tides from March to August each year. Their run is timed to come just after the peak of the tide. The fishes bury their eggs, after fertilization, in the sand just above the water mark, coming in with one wave and often moving out with the next. Two weeks later, during the next full or new moon another series of high tides releases the young, which have developed meanwhile in the buried eggs.

The head region of a lamprey (*Petromyzon*) showing the circular sucking mouth and the gill openings. Photo by Gerhard Marcuse.

Long-distance migrations

The best known migrators among the fishes are the eels (European eel, *Anguilla anguilla* and American eel, *A. rostrata*, for example) and the Atlantic and Pacific salmon *(Salmo salar* and *Oncorhynchus* species, respectively). They represent two major types of spawning migration, the *catadromous* fishes, including not only the freshwater eels, but also some gobies and southern hemisphere Galaxiidae, that make their way from fresh water to spawn in the ocean, and the *anadromous* migrants, represented by the shad *(Alosa sapidissima)* and the lamprey *(Petromyzon)* in addition to the salmons, that ascend rivers and lakes from the ocean in order to deposit their eggs in fresh water. Many other fishes migrate long distances to follow their food supply or for breeding purposes. The present holder of the long-distance record for a tagged fish is a bluefin tuna *(Thunnus thynnus)* that migrated from Cat Cay in the Bahamas to Bergen, Norway, a distance of 7,700 km, in 50 days, at a minimum average speed of 154 km/day. A striped marlin *(Tetrapturus audax)* made it from Baja California to Hawaii (5,680 km) at a minimum average speed of 62 km/day. Tagged Pacific salmon have been known to travel up to 3,600 km at an average minimum speed of 60 km/day. European eels must travel some 5,000 km from their breeding grounds in the Sargasso Sea, but they take three years for their journey; obviously they are not in a hurry. American eels don't have to travel as far and thus only take two years.

Marlins (*Makaira*) are oceanic fishes capable of swimming long distances at a fast speed. Photo by Walter Deas.

Some species of *Prochilodus* traverse a very extensive length of the Amazon River during their lifetime. Photo by Dr. Herbert R. Axelrod.

Carps like this *Erimyzon succetta* typically move upstream to spawn. Photo by Aaron Norman.

Flyingfishes (*Cypselurus*) can travel 35 miles per hour. Photo by Dr. Shih-chieh Shen.

Sea robins (*Trigla*) are slow travelers in comparison to some pelagic fishes like the jacks and mackerels. Photo by Gunter Senfft.

The discovery of the breeding grounds of the eel was an exciting event in the history of science. The migration of adult eels to the sea and the return of the young eels, known as elvers, to the streams and rivers they must ascend to grow to adulthood, and where they spend the greatest part of their lives, were well known. But the location of their breeding grounds was a complete mystery. The first break came in 1896 when two Italians, Grassi and Calandruccio, made the startling discovery that the eel's larval stage had been known for a long time, but that the leaf-shaped, transparent little creatures, known as leptocephali, had been classified as an entirely different species. The complete solution of the mystery had to wait until 1906, when the results of an international concerted effort, led by the Danish biologist and oceanographer Dr. Johann Schmidt, showed that leptocephali became smaller and smaller the closer they were picked up to the Sargasso Sea, an area of the Atlantic

ocean, north of the West Indies and south of Bermuda. The conclusion was inescapable, the breeding ground of the eel was right there in the Sargasso Sea. There is plenty of mystery left to the story. No one knows for sure what happens to the adults after spawning. There may be two separate populations, an European and an American, or the difference between the two species, mainly an average of seven and a half more vertebrae in the European eel, may develop only during the additional year that the European leptocephalus spends in the Atlantic. And finally, there is still another breeding ground to be discovered, for there are eel species that ascend the rivers of the countries of the western Pacific and the Indo-pacific region, sometimes by the millions. These fishes, as adults, slip into the Pacific to spawn at some destination unknown.

Eels do not ascend the rivers of the American Pacific coast, but great numbers of the anadromous Pacific salmon *(On-*

corhynchus) species do. The accuracy of their return journey is legendary. Each fish attempts to return to the stream in which it spent its early life, overcoming all obstacles on the way. It is guided by its memory of some characteristics of the environment of these few weeks spent in the vicinity of its hatching, before it starts its downstream migration. Eggs may be taken from a ripe female and fertilized in a hatchery. When released in a suitable stream, a migrating population can be established which will return to their new breeding grounds at the appropriate time, while ignoring entirely the stream where its parents originated. Pacific salmon, such as the coho *(Oncorhynchus kisutch)* have even been successfully stocked in Atlantic coast streams. It scarcely needs to be pointed out that this flexibility of route selection argues convincingly against the explanation of salmon migration on a purely innate basis. Pacific salmon make the upstream journey only once and die exhaustedly soon after spawning. Atlantic salmon *(Salmo salar)* ascend their home stream year after year and thus may be expected to learn more about their migration route with each trip.

Much has been written about the salmon migrating to their spawning grounds, but the downstream journey of the young fry is even more remarkable. After all, the adult has at least made the trip once in his life; the young have to travel to the ocean all on their own, often through very complex systems of lakes and streams. The young sockeye salmon *(Oncorhynchus nerka)* has been studied extensively. The fry emerge from their incubation area in gravel beds of fast moving streams. They must then travel downstream, upstream or a combination of both to lake nursery areas. Each local population, when tested, made the appropriate response by going against a current, with a current or both with and against a current. The response was so specific that hybrids between different populations showed intermediate behavior.

Size and age of the fry did not matter, but temperature and light influenced the intensity of the response. Sharp temperature increases often were followed by peak numbers of fry leaving their incubation area, but did not influence the direction of their travels. Fry performed well in darkness, but needed light to maneuver through high velocity currents.

Preference tests showed that smell played an important role in orientation. Water from different sources could be discriminated as shown by the behavior of newly hatched alevins who preferred water from the stream in which they had incubated, while a little older fry and fingerlings preferred water from the lake to which they had to migrate. Fry with their sense of smell made inoperative by closing off their nasal openings were disoriented.

Temperature plays a major role in the migration of the shad *(Alosa sapidissima)*. This large member of the herring family ascends the major rivers of the Atlantic coast to spawn in a pattern that varies seasonally. Shad runs occur in January in the St. Johns River in Florida, in February shad reach the Savannah River in Georgia and so on systematically up the coast until they arrived at the Hudson and Connecticut Rivers in May and the St. John River in Canada in June. After spawning, they congregate in the Gulf of Maine and the Bay of Fundy until it is time to make their return trip south, beginning in October and timed to arrive off the coast of Florida in January. Each local population ascends the river in which it was spawned during the course of this 2400 mile annual trek. The controlling factor, as tagging studies have shown, was the water temperature. Shad entered the rivers of Florida when the water temperature had fallen to the range of 13 to 16 degrees C. and followed the warming waters north with rising temperatures in Spring. Shad showed a preferred range of 13 to 18 degrees C. By sampling water temperature, the arrival of the spawning run could be predicted. Con-

Tarpons are large marine fish which commonly enter fresh water areas periodically. Shown above is *Megalops cyprinoides*, a small herring-like tarpon from Asian waters. Photo by Dr. Shih-chieh Shen

Brook trout, *Salvelinus fontinalis*, are permanent residents of freshwater streams and rivers of the United States. However, sea-run forms are found in the coast of Canada. Photo by Dr. D. Terver, Nancy Aquarium.

Leporinus and a few other fishes move upstream in the Amazon during flood conditions. Photo by Dr. Herbert R. Axelrod.

Mosquitofish (*Gambusia affinis*) scoot for the shallows along the shoreline to escape predators. The direction of the shoreline appears to be fixed by using the sun as a compass. Photo by Rudolf Zukal.

firmation of this correlation also came from the Pacific coast, where shad had been introduced in the Sacramento River in 1871 and have spread widely in the intervening years. Counts of shad ascending the Columbia River are taken at the Bonneville Dam fish ladders. They show a peak when water temperature ranges from 16.5 to 19 degrees C.

How do the fish find the mouth of the river they must ascend? Scientists have attached ultrasonic transmitters to the fish and have tracked individuals in their approach run off the Connecticut River. In open water they appear to make use of tidal currents. Since tides change approximately every six hours, the fishes reverse swimming direction every six hours too. But against the incoming tide they swam only fast enough to counteract the current, effectively staying in place. The outgoing tide, on the other hand, caused them to swim faster than the current, thus moving them closer to shore. Reduced salinity as they near the river mouth and chemical cues from the river water play a role in precise location of their route. Some extra time is spent in the tidal reaches of the river, presumably to allow time for the physiological changes needed to adjust from a salt water to a fresh water environment.

The principles governing long-range migration seem to be similar for catadromous fishes. The young European eels must ascend fresh water streams they have never seen. At the end of their three year journey as leptocephali, which they probably completed passively by drifting in the Gulf Stream, they metamorphose in August or September at the edge of the continental slope, before entering the English Channel or the North Sea. They spend some time in further passive travel as elvers, before taking a more active role in late winter and early spring. Now they become sensitive to the odor of freshwater streams emptying into the North Sea. In laboratory experiments they preferred natural fresh water over sea water. Filtering over charcoal filters removed the attractive factor from the fresh water. When natural fresh water was introduced into the apparatus, the elvers swam actively against the current, in some cases before the salinity recorder could register the change; when salinity increased, they sank to the bottom of the test tank and clung to the sandy surface. When the outgoing tide became too strong to make any headway, the elvers also sought shelter at the bottom. On a simulated incoming tide of high velocity these elvers now allowed themselves to be swept along or actively swum with the current. This passive mode of transport may perhaps be regarded as continuation of the mode of travel they had experienced as leptocephali and young elvers before coming under the influence of estuarine waters.

Homing

Fishes are really homebodies. They normally prefer to live in a restricted portion of their environment which they know well and which provides them with all the food and shelter they need. When displaced from this home area, they attempt to return as fast as possible. Sunfishes (*Lepomis*) have been estimated to have a home range of 100 to 200 feet; basses (*Micropterus*) have a range of 200 to 400 feet. Inhabitants of coral reefs select a small portion of the reef as their home territory and defend it against all comers. It is quite likely that the suitability of fishes for aquarium culture depends on the fact that many species are satisfied with their miniature world and distressed by being moved into a new environment. The ill effects of moving a fish to a new tank may, in fact, be partially due to the disruption of the bond that had been established between the fish and its home grounds.

Homing is well developed, both in migratory and non-migratory species. For example, American eels (*Anguilla rostrata*) were tagged and transplanted from the Shediac River 50 miles north to the

Histrio histrio, the sargassum fish, conceals itself very successfully in clumps of brown seaweed, *Sargassum.* Although poor swimmers they are able to reach a wider area of distribution; carried to distant places as flotsam subject to wind and ocean currents. Photo courtesy of the New York Zoological Society.

Parrotfishes, *Scarus coelestinus*, top, and *Scarus guacamia*, middle, were found capable of using sun navigation to find their way back to their coral reef territory. Photo by Dr. John E. Randall.

Young channel catfish, *Ictalurus punctatus*, were not able to home to an odor trail. Photo by Aaron Norman.

Kouchibouguacis River, both in New Brunswick, Canada. Four eels homed successfully all the way, others were captured half way to their goal. None were recovered north of the Kouchibouguacis.

Smell and vision play a role in the homing of cutthroat trout *(Salmo clarki)*, a study of their behavior in Yellowstone National Park revealed. Mature trout migrate from Yellowstone Lake into tributary streams to spawn. Fish were removed from their spawning beds and displaced various distances downstream. As in all these experiments, only a small percentage was actually recovered, but these constituted a significant proportion of the total number released. In one experiment 532 fishes were displaced, 135 or 26.4% homed, 23 or 4.5% strayed and 281 or 52.8% were unaccounted for. In another release 29 out of 71 fishes (40.9%) returned to the same area from which they had been taken, 18 others (25.4%) returned to the close vicinity of the home area, which had often been taken over by another pair in the meantime. Only nine fishes (12.7%) strayed and 14 (19.7%) were unaccounted for. Plugging of the external nasal opening or blinding the trout resulted in poorer performance, both in the number that homed and the longer time it took them to return, but neither one of these senses proved absolutely essential. Both visual and olfactory cues seemed to play a part in homing, yet these trout could apparently compensate for the loss of one sense by relying on the other.

Some of the pioneer experiments in this area were carried out by Professor Arthur Hasler and his students at the University of Wisconsin.* Green sunfish *(Lepomis cyanellus)* and largemouth bass *(Micropterus salmoides)* were captured near shore, marked by clipping their fins in a distinctive pattern and released in the center of

* For a fascinating review of this and other studies, the interested reader is referred to: A. D. Hasler, Underwater guideposts, Madison, Wis.: U. Wisconsin Press, 1966.

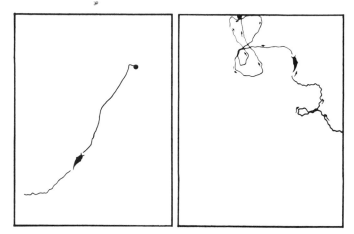

Traces made by bullheads following an attractive taste, in still water (left) and in slowly flowing water (right). (From Bardach, J.E., Chemo-Sensory perception in the bullhead. University of Michigan Research News, Vol. 17, No. 9, 1967.) (See Page 262.)

The experimental setup for observing a bullhead's path toward an attractive taste. The aimless trace at the center of the photograph shows the course of the bullhead's random swimming before he tasted the attractant. The almost straight trace at upper left shows the course he is following toward the source of the attractant. The trace was photographed by ultraviolet light; just before the fish reached the source, the whole setup was photographed by the light of a flash bulb.

their home lake. A very large percentage of recaptures took place at the same end of the lake where the fish had originally been found. Successful homing occurred even after a period of several winter months that the fish spent in the middle of the lake while the shallow portions were frozen solid. Tagged with a bobber attached by a nylon thread to the posterior fin, fish could be traced individually. In the preponderance of cases, and especially during the peak of the breeding season "they returned in a nearly direct route, and with dispatch, to their nests." When put into an adjacent pond, however, they were not motivated to move directionally, but swum "aimlessly." The shoreline and local bottom contours were not visible to the fish, but the sun was at no time invisible. Hasler therefore thought it likely that the fish were using the sun as compass, as long as they recognized the water as familiar.

Salmon homing, often considered the epitome of homing behavior, is indeed a remarkable achievement, although it is somewhat different from the behaviors discussed up to now. Return to the home stream involves the accurate retention of a location over a long period of time. It is puzzling how this learning takes place, as there is no obvious reinforcement available at the time of the emergence of the fry to account for the subsequent recognition and preference for home stream waters. Nevertheless, it is clear today that chemical cues are learned during the fingerling and smolt phases of salmon development, that this information is retained for several years and that it is used eventually to locate the home stream. Hasler's research team has reared fingerling salmon in an environment scented with a unique chemical, marked this and a control group, and released both groups into Lake Michigan. Eighteen months later many more previously exposed than unexposed salmon were drawn to a stream scented with the same odor. Tracking of salmon equipped with ultrasonic transmitters showed that only adults,

exposed to the scent as fingerlings, remained in the migratory route. Finally, exposed adults showed characteristic high amplitude potentials when their brain waves (EEG) were recorded at the same time as scented water was introduced into their olfactory organ.

The return of the adult salmon then appears to be guided by olfactory cues, once it approaches the estuary of its native stream closely enough for odor cues to become effective, but what is its guide on the high seas? Many intriguing ideas have been advanced to account for its long-range navigational system, but as yet the feat is still clouded in mystery. The guidance mechanism does not have to be terribly accurate, it seems. Professor Saul Saila of the University of Rhode Island has simulated the homeward trek of the Pacific salmon with the aid of a computer model. By utilizing known facts about distance traveled and speed of migration from recovery of tagged animals, and allowing the salmon a limited amount of time at the coast to find its way, he determined that a small deviation from randomness would bring his model in correspondence with actual return rates.

Navigation

A wide range of navigational systems has been shown to be available to fishes. Any or all may be utilized in a particular situation. In addition, the future will undoubtedly bring the discovery of new methods of navigation, for present knowledge does not seem adequate to account for all the facts that have been ascertained up to now.

VISION. The characteristics of underwater optics make visual direction finding much more difficult than the equivalent problem in air. Nevertheless, most fishes have well-developed eyes and undoubtedly make use of them in orientation and navigation. Light becomes attenuated rapidly even when the water is clear, which it often is not. Local features are undoubtedly recognized by fishes and serve as landmarks, as demonstrated, for example, by the study of the goby, *Bathygobius soporator*, jumping from one tidepool to another at low tide, after having surveyed the layout during high tide, mentioned in the discussion of learning. Blinded trout and salmon homed when displaced from their spawning grounds, but often not as well as normal control animals. But only in shallow waters and in the top layers can the fish eye be expected to discriminate significant detail. And on the high seas, the only possible clue could be the main direction of wave fronts.

The alternative is orientation by some celestial body, the sun, the moon or the stars. Direct time-compensated direction finding has been demonstrated in a number of species in laboratory experiments like the one described in the section on biorhythms. Tracking of displaced white bass (*Roccus chrysops*) in Lake Mendota, Wisconsin, indicated that the sun's position was utilized by some of the fishes. Downstream migration of young sockeye salmon (*Oncorhynchus nerka*) through Babine Lake in British Columbia, Canada, also seemed to depend on the sun's position. Two species of parrot fishes (*Scarus guacamaia* and *S. coelestinus*) seemed to be capable of using sun navigation to return to their coral reef territory. Even the tiny mosquito fish (*Gambusia affinis*), which is well-known to aquarists, uses the sun's position for orientation. Under natural conditions mosquito fish scoot for the shallows along the shoreline to escape larger predators, such as the various sunfishes and bass that prey on them. The direction of the shoreline appears to be fixed by celestial navigation. Orientation failed under completely overcast skies, in diffuse light and after fish were kept in darkness for 72 hours.

Recent experiments have demonstrated that fishes may use not only the sun's position directly, but that some of them may also use the polarization pattern of both the sky and of underwater sunlight. A number of fishes have been examined since the first discoveries were made by

T. H. Waterman of Yale University, who found underwater polarization an effective cue for the halfbeaks *Zenarchopterus dispar* and *Z. buffoni* at Palau in the south Pacific. The well-known freshwater halfbeak *Dermogenys pusillus* has also been tested in aquariums where it has indicated a capacity to distinguish the plane of polarization of artificially polarized light. Underwater light is polarized at depths where direct observation of the sun is impossible, so it may be an important navigational aid. On the other hand, there is at present no good explanation of the mechanism by which the fish eye or an extra-optic system of receptors could resolve the plane of polarization.

AUDITION. Whereas light is quickly attenuated by water and thus does not always constitute a dependable aid to navigation and odors tend to be transmitted slowly and diffusely, acoustic vibrations would appear to be an ideal channel for underwater orientation. Nonetheless, scientists know very little of the use fishes may make of auditory information for navigational purposes. Even echolocation has not as yet been convincingly demonstrated in fishes, although aquatic mammals, such as whales and dolphins, have well-established echoranging equipment. A possible exception should be noted. The sea catfish, *Galeichthys felis*, is a common estuarine species of the southeastern United States coast, and has long been known as a sound producer. Among the various types of sound it has available is one consisting of low frequency pulse bursts of 5 to 10 milliseconds duration. The component frequencies of these sounds vary from less than 100 Hz to over 1500 Hz. These bursts of sound seem to be modulated when obstacles are approached. The catfishes abruptly turn aside before reaching the barrier. When transparent obstacles were introduced into the tank, there was an immediate, temporary increase of these sounds. Blinded animals also avoided barriers with almost complete success, even from the first moment of introduction. These sounds are in the fish's hearing range and may well be used in orientation, although at present the evidence is indirect.

Sound localization has also been studied in the Hawaiian squirrelfishes *Myripristis berndti* and *M. argyromus*. Observations were made in a large pond open to a bay, of movements toward one of two underwater loudspeakers emitting squirrelfish alarm calls. Localization consisted of fish choosing between two speakers, one of which was broadcasting sounds made by captive squirrelfish in response to a predator, namely a moray eel. The animals approached the loudspeaker, but appeared to respond primarily to "near-field," rather than acoustic far-field effects.

While the utilization of acoustic signals as navigational aids is still an unresolved question, there is no doubt that the lateral line system, which is closely associated with the auditory capacity in fishes, plays an important role in orientation. This system is useful in localizing objects at a distance and in detecting obstacles. It may also help in sensing water currents.

OLFACTION. It is clear today, as the studies of salmon migration have revealed, for example, that chemical cues play a large role in guiding the salmon during their spawning run, as they ascend their home stream. What is the source of the odors that help the fish to distinguish their stream from all the other alternatives? Bluntnose minnows *(Hyborhynchus notatus)* were able to distinguish between water in which different plant species have been raised. Recognition of the home stream seems to depend on these subtle differences

Nurse shark (*Ginglymostoma cirratum*) followed the gradient of chemical stimulation. Photo by Robert Straughan.

Hawaiian squirrelfish (*Myripristis berndti*) used in sound localization experiments. Photo by Dr. Herbert R. Axelrod.

in minute quantities of dissolved substances. Attempts are now in progress to train salmon to home to an artificial odor and to use this substance to guide salmon around such obstacles as dams and intake screens of power plants.

A certain amount of time must be spent in a given location, before fishes develop a preference for the smell of a body of water. Ten day old fry of channel catfish (*Ictalurus punctatus*) and silver shiners (*Notropis photogenis*) did not attempt to seek the arm of a Y-shaped channel carrying odor cues from their home waters, but adult shiners and goldfish did. Their preference was not necessarily stable over long periods of time, however, being lost after 30 days by the goldfish and 60 days by the shiners.

The effects of scents of various kinds on the activity of several species of fish has been reported. The lamprey *Petromyzon marinus* reacted to the odor of trout, for example, by a sudden, typical change of its swimming pattern. The nurse shark *Ginglymostoma cirratum*, in one experiment, swam in a pattern that could best be described by a logarithmic spiral. It seemed to follow the gradient of chemical stimulation, seeking out its source. The lemon shark *Negaprion brevirostris*, on the other hand, merely seemed to orient against the current, when his nose detected the scent of potential food. Of course, this behavior will often lead to the source of the smell, as it would have to be carried by the current. The recognition of these two different types of orientation to odor appears to resolve some of the long-standing contradictions among studies of feeding and attack patterns of sharks.

The efficiency of the olfactory system of fishes has led to the suggestion to utilize this ability to detect chemical pollutants. Minnows may be trained to detect the presence of phenol, a common pollutant, by teaching them to swim toward water containing phenol in a choice situation. Another approach uses a conditioning technique in which goldfish hit a circular underwater target to get reinforced with *Tubifex* worms. A base rate of responding is eventually established. The introduction of organic mercury into the water changes

The taste buds of the brown bullhead, *Ictalurus nebulosus*, are concentrated in the barbels. However, other parts of the body are equipped with taste organs also. Photo by G.J.M. Timmerman.

the rate of responding significantly, thus serving as a sensitive warning signal for pollution.

GUSTATION. Taste has generally not been considered a long range aid to navigation, but this idea needs revision. Catfish and loaches have well-equipped taste receptors and apparently they use them in orientation. Brown and yellow bullheads *(Ictalurus nebulosus* and *I. natalis)* have thousands of external taste buds all over the body, although, of course, the main concentration is found in the barbels. These taste organs can be used in true gradient fashion to locate the source of a scent. No current is needed to carry the odor. Elimination of vision and olfaction did not impair the bullhead's accurate homing abilities.

TEMPERATURE. The temperature dependence of the shad's migration indicates that temperature gradients play a role in navigational guidance of fishes. Controlled experiments have been carried out on the effect of temperature on the activity patterns of the bluefish *(Pomatomus saltatrix)*. Once they are acclimatized to a stable tem-

perature, both increases and decreases in temperature resulted in an increase in overall swimming activity, at least until stressful extremes were reached. Similar findings have been reported for the Atlantic salmon *(Salmo salar)* and the mackerel *(Scomber scomber)*. Obviously, further study is needed, but these increases in swimming activity in an unlimited ocean would presumably carry the fish along in an optimum temperature zone. It would also explain how fishes can follow a discontinuity in water temperature, such as the Gulf Stream.

INERTIAL GUIDANCE. When a rocket flies to the moon, it is given a set of instructions and aimed at the particular point in the sky where the moon will be at the time the rocket is to reach its goal. Any deviations from the correct course are sensed by the navigational system and automatically corrected. This inertial guidance system is also successfully applied to fly airplanes on automatic pilot and to keep ocean liners on a preselected course. It has occurred to a number of scientists that the navigation of migrating animals could be based on the same principle. The obvious candidate for such a system in vertebrates would be their semicircular canals. There is some evidence that fishes are able to compensate for deviations in one direction by making an equal number of turns in the opposite direction, in the absence of other cues. Goldfish *(Carassius auratus)* were monitored in an automated observation tank constructed by Professor Herman Kleerekoper and his associates at Texas A & M University. Embedded in the bottom of the tank was an array of 1936 photocells, illuminated by uniform overhead lights. Any movement was tracked by the interruption of the light path as the fishes moved around the tank. A computer stored this information and analyzed the data. The movement of a particular fish would not show a consistent turning in any one direction, followed by turns in the opposite direction, but computer analysis over 24 hours showed that over a long time period right and left turns evened out, so that a constant heading would have been maintained by a fish in open waters. Analysis showed that this effect was not just due to random motions balancing out, but to a deliberate compensation of turn directions. Should this mechanism be confirmed in other experiments, it would mean that fishes could select a direction by means of some external reference point, then guide their movement by sensing deviations from their course and making corrective turns whenever necessary on the basis of their inertial guidance system.

ELECTRICAL AND MAGNETIC FIELDS. Potentially, the earth's magnetic field and the electrical currents generated by fishes moving through the magnetic field, provide a ready made navigational aid. Evidence for the perception of magnetic fields in fishes is completely lacking, however, at this time. Sensitivity to electrical currents is well established in some fishes but its use in navigation is presently obscure. The main problem lies in the minuteness of the induced currents, which are several magnitudes below the established thresholds for electrical forces in fishes.

The Atlantic salmon *(Salmo salar)* and the American eel *(Anguilla rostrata)* have been tested in weak magnetic and electric fields, by the very sensitive technique of heart rate conditioning. Neither eels nor salmon appeared to respond to the magnetic fields. The eels did, however, give some evidence of responding to the electric field and a trend in the same direction was shown by the salmon. Obviously, further study of this capacity is indicated. Sharks and rays *(Scyliorhinus canicula* and *Raja clavata)* have been found even more sensitive than teleosts and may well have the sensitivity and frequency range to use the electric fields they generate when swimming through the earth's magnetic field. They may possibly also utilize induced electrical fields to detect passive drift with ocean currents or as an indication of local features, such as coastlines. It is also conceivable that the mormyrids and related weakly electrical fishes could use their electrical sense for navigation, in addition to their proven ability to use it for electrolocation. Obviously, many questions still remain, hopefully the future will bring us some answers.

A final word to the reader

This account of why fishes do what they do has been written without appealing to any of the technical terms, such as motive, drive or instinct, that scientists generally employ to "explain" why fishes (or other animals or even people) do what they do. It is the writer's contention that these terms at best are used as a shorthand description of certain observed relationships and at worst as a cover for our ignorance.

Ultimately this ignorance has its roots in the basic paradox of any behavioral analysis. A fish lives in his own world. The way the fish perceives his environment, what it thinks, feels or experiences are forever closed off from the outside observer. For an extreme case, think of how a fish would interpret the signals of his lateral line system or the cues to orientation that apparently are based on his own electrical field.

The human observer is also locked into his own world. That is the other side of the paradox. We can only interpret behavior in terms of our own experience. When we say that a fish sees, hears, courts, learns or orients, we are using essentially human terms to describe fish behavior. The fish couldn't care less. But we can only think in terms that are familiar to us. Congenitally blind children, for example, can recognize objects very well by touch. When through a miracle of surgery their sight is restored, they are completely at a loss to recognize these same familiar objects by sight. Previous description cannot replace the actual experience. These children cannot think in visual terms without having had some acquaintance with the looks of things.

Lacking the ability to turn ourselves into a fish, we must be satisfied with coming as close as we can to the world of fishes. That is not as difficult as it sounds. We share the same biological heritage, in fact "relatively" speaking, we are not far apart in the scheme of evolution. And there are benefits to be gained. Observing fish behavior broadens our experience. It places human behavior in its proper perspective. And, besides, it is fun to watch fishes in their natural surroundings and in an aquarium.

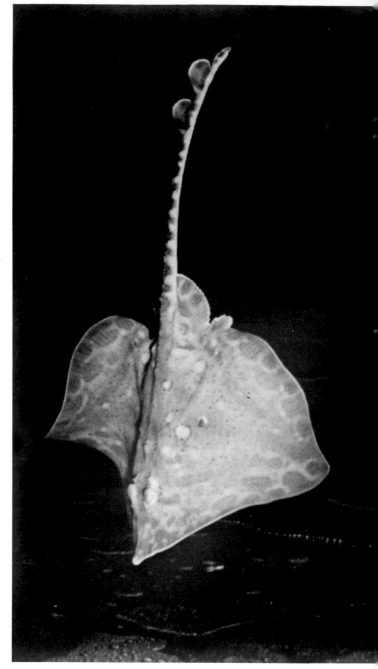

The thornback ray, *Raja clavata*, has been found capable of detecting a homogeneous alternating electrical field of 0.01 microvolts per centimeter. Photo by Gerhard Marcuse.

A BIOGRAPHICAL NOTE

Helmut E. Adler earned a Ph.D. in comparative psychology from Columbia University in 1952. He is a professor of psychology at Yeshiva University in New York, a research associate in animal behavior at The American Museum of Natural History and has been a consultant to the New York Aquarium. He is the author or co-author of *Bird Behavior* and *Bird Life (for young people)* and the editor and co-editor of *Orientation: Sensory Basis* and *Comparative Psychology at Issue*. He has been an enthusiastic tropical fish hobbyist since an early age. In recent years, keeping several large tropical fish tanks in his home was also enjoyed by his wife, Leonore, and was educational as well for his children, Barry, Beverly and Evelyn.

Further reading

Aronson, L.R. 1957. Reproductive and parental behavior. *In* M. E. Brown (ed.), *The physiology of fishes*, II, pp. 271–304. New York, Academic Press.

Baerends, G. P. 1957. Fish Behavior. *In* M. E. Brown (ed.), *The physiology of fishes*, II, pp. 229–269. New York, Academic Press.

Baerends, G. P. 1971. The ethological analysis of fish behavior. *In* Hoar, W. S. & Randall, D. J. (eds.), *Fish physiology*, pp. 279–370. New York, Ademic Press.

Breder, C. M., Jr. & D. E. Rosen. 1966. *Modes of reproduction in fishes*. Neptune City, N.J., T.F.H.

Bünning, E. 1967. *The physiological clock*. New York, Springer.

Gleitman, H. & P. Rozin. 1971. Learning and memory. *In* Hoar, W. S. & Randall, D. J. (eds.), *Fish physiology*, pp. 191–278. New York, Academic Press.

Hasler, A. D. 1966. *Underwater guideposts*. Madison, Wis., U. Wisconsin Press.

Ingle, D. (ed.). 1968. *The central nervous system and fish behavior*. Chicago, U. Chicago Press.

Lagler, K. F., J. E. Bardach & R. R. Miller. 1962. *Ichthyology*. New York, John Wiley & Sons.

Marshall, N. B. 1971. *Explorations in the life of fishes*. Cambridge, Mass., Harvard Univ. Press.

Ray, C. & E. Ciampi. 1956. *The underwater guide to marine life*. New York, A. S. Barnes & Co.

Schultz, L. P. 1948. *The ways of fishes*. Neptune City, N.J., T.F.H.

INDEX

Page numbers in **bold** face refer to illustrations.